You've Been Lied To...

Peter,
It's great
getting to know you!
Let's keep living
real & spreading
the truth,

Hank
Hayes

YOU'VE BEEN LIED TO...

THE UNTOLD TRUTH ABOUT MAINSTREAM ALCOHOL AND ADDICTION TREATMENT PROGRAMS AND THE SECRETS ON HOW TO ELIMINATE THE PROBLEM FOR GOOD

BY HANK HAYES

PUBLISHED BY LEKOTON+2

Library of Congress Cataloging-in-Publication Data
Hayes, Hank
You've Been Lied To...The Untold Truth about Mainstream Alcohol and Addiction Programs and the Secrets on How to Eliminate the Problem for Good.

ISBN 13:978-1463702397
ISBN 10:1463702396
LCCN2011913753
Printed in the United States of America
First Edition

Interior artwork by Anna Smedley
Front cover photography by Eyvind C. Boyesen

DEDICATION AND ACKNOWLEDGEMENTS

. . . .

Wow, I can't believe we got it done babe. How totally cool!!! Without question I have to start my dedication off with huge thanks to my beautiful wife Melissa, for without her endless help, guidance and love this project would not be brought to life. She has talked me down, pumped me up and supported me through everything, it's a wonder how a marriage can endure so much yet still have more magic than when we first met. Thank you for being there, for never giving up and for always believing in me, I love you forever Babe...

I need to be careful because I know I could write pages on those I want to dedicate thanks to for their positive influence in my life that have given me the courage to look past what everybody else is focused on and find the truth. I have to thank my Mom and Dad. These folks were trailblazers and role models who instilled in me beliefs that if you don't stand for something you'll fall for anything. They taught me to respect all people, to not take shit from anybody, and to make your dreams come true.

I want to thank my kids, Legend, Braxton, Dakota, Raina and Cheyenne, for proving to me every day that walking angels do exist, for constantly teaching me about life and showing me what best friends truly are.

I want to thank my first real mentor Bill Bancroft for teaching me numerous invaluable lessons. Thank you SO much Big Bill for showing me what it takes to make it—the big and the small.

I want to say thanks to my father in law Eyvind Boyesen. He is proof that God does live within people. Thank you for all you've given to the world and the legacy you've left behind. Within this thanks I want to shout out to Momma Joy and the rest of the dozens of Boyesens and my extended family. These guys know the meaning of family, big time!

I want to thank my special friends Jennifer Nunnikhoven, Tim Heaslet and Ray Fabela for being a cheering section, a sounding board and true friends. True friends tell you no when you're selling yes, true friends tell you that you can do it when you think you can't, true friends believe in your dreams. Thanks guys!

Back in the mid-1980s I was turned on to Tony Robbins and he awakened the giant within, from that time forward so many personal development leaders, authors and educators have taught, motivated and inspired me to go get the life that I wanted and do my best to be a role model to others.

These great men and women are in no special order but have gotten deep within my soul and for that I must acknowledge them. Mr. Jim Rohn, Les Brown, Brian Tracy, Dr. Wayne Dyer, Jack Canfield, Darren Hardy, Brendan Burchard, Joel Osteen, John Maxwell, the men and women in the U.S. Armed Forces, T. Harv Eker, Dr. Stanton Peele, Dr. Tom Horvath, Bruce Lee, Kevin Trudeau, Chris Widener, John Assaraf, Dr. Daniel Amen, Charlie "Tremendous" Jones and John Salvaggio. There are so many others that have positively influenced me. However I must stop somewhere.

Thank you all for what you have done for me. You have my word I will carry the torch with the same passion and intent.

Hank Hayes
Son of Lewis Hayes and Eyvind Boyesen
Godspeed forever...

CONTENTS

······································

PART ONE

GETTING TO THE TRUTH

THE OPENER

. . . .

My name is Hank Hayes and this is my personal journal which turned into a massive research paper and finally this book from over 17 years of being involved in the recovery culture. But most importantly it's about the path I and numerous others took to attain an everyday state of sobriety, unbelievable well-being and true freedom.

I'm thinking about my Dad, who was the best man I ever knew. He respected all people for who they were, where they were. He would always say to me, "Do the best you can from where you are with what you've got." I don't say this because he was my Dad. I say this because it's just the way it was and if he were alive today in the physical world, I know he would be so proud of me and tell me personally, "Great job kid!"

As I sit here writing I'm thinking, How did I ever let my life get as bad as it did? I was a locked down, solitarily confined inmate in a prison of my own creation, built of my own crappy destructive thinking, my negative mindset. And in the end alcohol and drugs became part of my everyday scheduling. Not too much was getting done without a plan of when I was going to use. Whether I knew it or not it was an integral part of my life. Even once in traditional recovery with years of sobriety, I was never truly comfortable or ever really free!

I'm here before you today to report I am totally free. I am a completely free man! Picture a guy standing on the highest mountain peak with arms outstretched yelling to the world and knowing in his heart of hearts he is free as a bird. That is me today, bound and chained to nothing. I can go anywhere I want, do anything I want and be whomever I want with ZERO threats, free to really live, and I do!

Within the pages of this book I share with you the lies that we've bought, hook line and sinker. I reveal the truth about the recovery industry and share how I and millions of others found a hidden path to sobriety (the one they don't want you to know about). Let me tell you, you don't have to spend countless hours going to meetings stuck with people you would otherwise never want to be with. You do not have to report to a sponsor, subject yourself to being brainwashed into thinking you have some trumped-up disease and basically forced to admit that you're powerless.

There is another way! A way that I and numerous others found that lasts, a repeatable process that is true and will give you freedom in every area of your life and beyond!

In this book we will provide you with the secret to an addiction-free life. We will give you the 5 keys to eliminating your or your loved one's addiction for good. However this book is so much more than the solution to addiction, it will open your eyes and provide a framework for a high-performance life.

In addition to this book we've concluded with 9 inspiring and surprising, true, sober short stories that vary greatly in life experience and content. These people's stories are raw, real and heartfelt and you will find yourself amazed and uplifted by how they found sobriety on their own without the mainstream industry.

Join us and make the shift to a life of total freedom!

INTRODUCTION

· ·

L ie: A false statement made with deliberate intent to deceive; an intentional untruth; a falsehood. During our lives we encounter so many little and sometimes not so little lies. We even tell some ourselves, with our own personal motives hiding behind them. But in the end, I'm sure you agree, the truth always makes things so much easier. Yes the truth will always set you free!

Picture a random Sunday night. My wife and I are sitting on the couch watching a movie when all of a sudden we hear a loud crash in the kitchen. Seconds later my youngest son comes sliding into the living room like Kramer from Seinfeld and says, "I didn't do anything!" My wife and I look at each other, roll our eyes and ask, "What did you break?" Then the confession comes...

That lie is fairly basic. But the next story example is a little more deceptive: My wife has a Chevy four-wheel drive which recently had the transmission rebuilt. Fifteen thousand miles into the new tranny we start having shifting problems again. I had my wife call the transmission shop to express our concerns and schedule an appointment. Being the great wife she is she brings the truck down to the shop for a diagnosis. They say the truck not only needs to have the transmission rebuilt again but also needs a tune-up and brakes all around ASAP.

Seems simple and straightforward right? Not! Generally every Saturday the wife and I swap cars and I get her truck cleaned and do a quick check of any car issues, oil level, brakes, radiator fluids, etc. The mechanic around the corner from us does all the regular/basic work, including brakes, tune-ups, etc, and happens to do a great job with small auto work, however doesn't do big jobs like transmissions.

I just happened to call my wife and she gave me the wonderful news. Bottom line, Joe's "honest" transmission shop was trying to take my wife and I for a long ride, lying and manipulating the whole way. They knew the brakes were fine; they were done only two weeks earlier along with a full tune-up by my neighborhood mechanic. They wanted my wife in and out of there before she could even think about it and would have padded the bill 1,200 bucks without touching the brakes. If I hadn't called on a fluke, we might have been totally lied to and stolen from and never known the difference. This also makes me wonder about the initial work they did.

It is these little life experiences that collectively add to our frustrations. When you visit a Doctor, put your trust in your child's teacher or go to a personal trainer, you expect that they have the best most current information and will implement the most effective program. You trust them, right? After all, they are the experts. It is no different for me and the millions of other people out there with a drinking or addiction issue who want help.

What I found was that the mainstream prescription and direction for recovery was not only unbelievably outdated but built on lies and designed to keep people sick and coming back for more so-called treatment. Would you enroll yourself or your wife, husband or child on a team, in a medical procedure or in an educational facility that had a 5% success record? Well that's what's happening to millions of people every day!

I know for me when it was time to enter the treatment and recovery period of my life I was so ready to get help! If it made any sense at all and frankly even if it didn't make sense I was going to follow direction to the letter. So off I went into the mainstream alcohol/drug treatment world and culture, trusting their methods to help me get better.

But after a few years I knew that something was wrong. What that was at the time wasn't clear and I couldn't put my finger on it but it was there. There was a great conflict within myself as I struggled along with the program and all the must do's required, never feeling that I was achieving anything close to what I was capable of.

Another few years went by and I started asking questions. Sometimes I got answers that sounded good but had little support, sometimes I got answers that sounded good and had no support. Other times I got answers that just made no sense whatsoever. In the beginning I believed what I was told, thinking the success records they were all talking about where true. I had no idea of the *real* truth!

This is where my quest really began, however I never thought it would reveal so much that I would be lead to tell the world about it. Through the years of frustration, struggling and yearning for a better way and after exhaustive research, the puzzle pieces slowly but surely fell into place. I found out for myself that we have been spoon-fed lie after lie, believing those lies, all along persevering only to waiver and then fail—again and again. I like so many others wondered over and over why this didn't work for me and what in the hell was wrong with me?

What I'm here to tell you is that it's not because of you that you haven't reached the level you've wanted. It's because of the bullshit we've been holding onto thinking that the mainstream treatment solution is the only way to get better. Well guess what. It is not!

There was no way I could let others stay in this mainstream treatment/recovery culture, continue to be manipulated and lied to and never know that much more powerful solutions exist.

I decided I would be the voice that blew the whistle! I would let everybody know how and where they were being lied to. But more importantly I would show them other brilliant options and resources that they can use, as hundreds of thousands of other people have, to move forward and beyond with their lives!

I would not leave them stuck with this idea in their heads that they have some disease they are doomed to deal with forever or that they have to go to meetings for the rest of their lives.

I found the following passage true for myself and saw the struggle others have had with this subconscious and deeply rooted fear...

Our deepest fear is not that we are inadequate. Our deepest fear is that we are powerful beyond measure. It is our light, not our darkness that most frightens us'...Your playing small doesn't serve the world... We are all meant to shine, as children do...It's not just in some of us; it's in everyone. And as we let our own light shine, we unconsciously give other people permission to do the same. As we're liberated from our own fear, our presence automatically liberates others.

– Marianne Williamson, *A Return to Love: Reflections on the Principles of "A Course in Miracles"*

Please join me on a journey of liberation, development of personal power and true freedom.

CHAPTER ONE

HOW AND WHY I CAME TO WRITE THIS BOOK

· ·

A s you read the following pages it's suggested that you not nec-
essarily look for similar feelings that I experienced but look for
an underlying theme, an unhealthy or incorrect way of handling
life that you or the someone that you're reading this for does or has done
in a recurring fashion. This will be not only the causative reason for the
current habit/abuse but the way out.

Something I would like to set straight for the record, you will not
hear a long drink and drug a-log story from me. My objective here is to
get right to it and create a baseline that you can relate to for yourself or
someone you love. I'll move on to clear the air and blow the whistle on the
lies that we've been told and many of us bought... *hook, line and sinker*.
Then I'll close with the art of attaining an exceptional life, PERIOD.

This is my story...

I was born in the early '60s in an all-Italian New York City neighborhood where earning street respect and being accepted was everything. I
had one thing going for me that would prove to create obstacles. I felt at
the time these were best handled by doing whatever it took to be liked
and not only fit in but stand out as a doer and a leader and gain that so
very needed respect.

I'm an African American born to a well-to-do family. My father was a highly educated man from Pittsburg, Pennsylvania, and my mother a prideful, classy southern bell from Bartow, Georgia.

Some of you might say, so what? What's the big deal? If you're at all familiar with New York City in the '60s there were certain lines that were not to be crossed as racial tensions were at an insane high back then and living as a black family on the Italian side was one of those lines you didn't cross without major issues. This was the start of my quest to be liked, fit in and stand out as a doer and a leader and get that respect.

You still may be saying I don't get it, what does this have to do with alcohol and drug abuse?

As I found out during my decade and a half in the conventional treatment world, alcohol and drug abusers have one of several things in common. We either never felt understood or we wanted to fit in and be a part of something. It may vary slightly but that was a common denominator with all the stories that were shared in group therapy, AA meetings, counseling sessions, books and in talking with other treatment centers or "program" peers one-on-one.

Although I didn't have my first drink until I was 14 years old, I was a master artist at escaping from reality. I did anything and everything possible to prove that I was a doer and would do unimaginable things at a young age to get attention and gain peer-level respect, a trait I carried right on into my teens and adulthood.

As we'll later see, just because one isn't drinking or drugging doesn't mean they don't have the exact same characteristics and/or behaviors as one who is. The good news is that we can get the exact same rewards and pleasures in a 100% safe, healthy and positive relationship, building ways to become mature, stable adults.

As a man who owns and operates a global company that provides some of the best combative tools and training to our nation's elite high-risk operators, we start off training by stating one thing. You want to operate from a proper baseline and the best baselines are those that are rooted in truth. If not, you risk not only your own life but the lives of your unit, team members and principles that you're protecting.

From my earliest memories I didn't feel accepted and unfortunately I wasn't. Most of my childhood was a fight to feel that I belonged. So either I was working to prove that I belonged or fighting to fit in and/or feel superior. This created the perfect storm for my non-ingested, self-abusive style behaviors. As I mentioned before most people I met in the recovery environment either didn't feel understood or wanted to fit in and feel like a part of something anyway they could—this was me to a tee!

I remember going to school at about age six and getting my lunch taken from me time after time until I finally got wise to it. We in the protection business call it pre-incident indicators. They are like tells in a poker game. Once wise to these tells at the tender age of 6, I would prepare myself for the inevitable, be ready to fight, and I did! I protected my Twinkies and peanut butter and jelly sandwiches at all costs, and I did a superior job of it. This was the start of a defensive reaction to most anybody or anything that gave me a feeling of being threatened in any way. I was always ready to fight and of course most physical altercations start verbally with anybody who is defensive or aggressive. Smart people back away and even smarter people avoid the situation totally. So guess who was left, the people who wanted trouble and the people who didn't know any better.

I didn't realize it at the time but I was setting up a pattern for myself that would follow me for decades. My burning desire to feel a part of or superior to was the other side.

For a while when I was young I was the last person picked for pickup games at the park. When that happened I would play my little heart out, because I knew if I didn't do an above-average job they wouldn't have me on the field again. I remember a time when the kids didn't pick me for a baseball game so when the game started I stood between the pitcher and catcher, arms crossed, blocking the game and utterly refused to move until a team finally picked me. During that game I hit more home runs and had more outstanding field plays then anyone else on either team. From that day on I was always picked for sports. It was instant gratification and I loved the feeling.

This was the start of a self-understanding that if I over-excelled and over-delivered I would be accepted, which I thought could be used in most all environments. I later found out this doesn't always work, not for a balanced quality life.

By the time I was 10 years old my main functioning state was "have attitude will travel" and "play harder, be better and you'll win them over." Remember earlier we talked about the best baselines being rooted in truth and if not there's a risk in not gaining a wholesome outcome. In my case I wasn't truly happy because I was NEVER just Hank. My fixed natural state was fight or flight, ready to defend or ready to excel and never understood what was lying beneath.

This went on to the extreme until the day presented itself to have alcohol without parental supervision. It was at the junior high school graduation party held at a gal's house from school who's parents were out of town; another perfect storm. Remember my functioning state "have attitude will travel" and "play harder, be better and you'll win them over."

So with a serious attitude I drank and danced harder and better than anyone; however, I didn't win anybody over. I threw up everywhere, the bulk of it in the pool—I had eaten nachos with cheese, sloppy joes and chicken wings... what a mess! To add insult to injury, when my Dad pulled up to get me and once in the car, I threw up all over the backseat and out the window for most of the way home. My Dad was *furious*!!! But you see he didn't understand...

Now after a first experience like that you would think I might have stopped or taken some notice, yes? Well I didn't. I know now that I had created my peer group, those that I was like-minded with for the most part. And with these people my behavior was no big deal. No big deal made, no big deal seen!

During that summer it was full-throttle partying from my perspective. I was hanging out with all the wrong people, going to all the wrong places and doing all the wrong things. My parents tried to show me that this type of lifestyle would lead nowhere fast. But my attitude was, hey they (my parents) don't understand what I'm going through!

Before we move on to high school please allow me to digress. My parents from birth always set the example for me that self-respect, respect for others and education were means to a great end. We traveled and vacationed to all the best places and I experienced cultural events such as plays, ballets, opera, sporting events and music.

I excelled greatly in most things that I did. Additionally I had a propensity for odder activities, things that most kids in our area of the country or of my race didn't generally do such as skateboarding, motocross, BMX, martial arts, surfing, hockey, auto body custom car builds, and hard rock guitar playing and I dated exclusively white girls. I had a great skill for making money which was modeled for me by my parents and the community that I grew up in. This in the years to come supported my rogue, self-destructive and abusive lifestyle.

During that summer I really sealed the deal on who I would spend most of my time with and who I would allow to be my greatest influencers. You've heard the saying "Birds of a feather flock together." Well I was flocking alright. There's another great saying: "You can't fly with the eagles if you hang with the turkeys." I don't know why anyone would want to do that anyway. Turkeys only take flight every now and again, make a bunch of noise, poop everywhere and walk around in it. Silly right? However this was exactly the life I was creating for myself. I did do a few great things now and again and for sure experienced some awesome things in life but I constantly found myself mucking around making a bunch of noise with messes everywhere for others and myself to clean up.

As high school started and progressed, I spent time solidifying the new me, building and strengthening relationships with whom I thought were the "in crowd." You see, in my mind I made them the in crowd because that's what I wanted them to be.

"We are what we think about and who we spend the most time with."

"As a man thinketh in his heart, so he is."
Proverbs 23:7

It couldn't have been more than three or four months into high school when I started experimenting with pot (a.k.a. the bag—for the remainder of this book all my references to any drugs will be called the bag). After an additional three or four months I was fairly heavily into my bag use and it was a daily way of life.

My underlying theme living itself out again "have attitude will travel" and "play harder, be better and you'll win them over," rebelling against school, parents and anybody who thought they could tell me better.

At this point I was in trouble all the time, fighting, chasing girls, playing my guitar and riding motorcycles. The bottle and bag were never far from hand. However all the while I was working hard, using my creativity, and I really believed I was still a good guy, so to speak.

Additionally to make matters worse my father was the principal of the local elementary school. This became a good and bad thing. My Dad was on me like white on rice. All of his teacher friends knew my every move but being a loving Dad he was always there to save me. He did a lot of saving so I got away with murder over and over and over; another reoccurring theme. Can you relate to any of this? If so, please stay with me; the facts and simple solutions in this book will blow your mind.

During my fourth year I was forced to go to a different high school, which was in a pretty rough neighborhood, but I didn't mind. Frankly there was just more there of what I wanted.

While in high school during the summer months I worked in an auto body shop and learned the craft well. Now if you know New York City you know what goes on in these body shops and it's not just painting cars. I'll leave the rest for your imagination.

While working at the body shop I met some people. These people were "well connected" as we say in New York. It wasn't long before I had my own body shop and was doing all the same things that I mentioned went on in New York City in these shops.

There I was, 21 years old, driving a big car, doing whatever I wanted and making all kinds of money with the backing and protection from, let's call them, my "friends."

Again, my underlying theme living itself out as "have attitude will travel" and "play harder, be better and you'll win them over."

I want to mention something that we'll discuss later in the book. It's a little scientific having to do with neuroplasticity which is the science of brain mapping. Webster's definition is: The brain's natural ability to form new connections in order to compensate for injury or changes in one's environment. This is how the brain functions at the neuron connectivity level and where that activity is located on the brain's surface. The statement I would like to refer to is "neurons that fire together wire together." In layman's terms, it's when there is an action that is done over and over and creates a strong pathway in the brain. When there's an action paired with high emotions, either positive or negative, it creates a superconnector, basically a habitual pattern of action.

As you can clearly see from my childhood years through to my early adult years the same theme played out. Therefore that neuropathway had been wired for a few decades from my formative years. As we move forward you'll see how this will continue to play itself out, taking on different forms and how I used this knowledge to get past the self-destructive and abusive lifestyle.

In my early adult years, with college not my most important endeavor, the people that I chose to be around and let influence me were the people that did what I did just as before. And as the saying goes "those that play together stay together." Little did I know but this was even more hardwiring happening on the backend.

In looking back I see that I created perfect environments to support what Hank wanted subconsciously. Work environments where I was in total control and earning the money needed to support my lifestyle. People in those environments who wouldn't say boo to me about what I was doing. This was the perfect cover for my odd hours, disappearing acts and plausible stories that at times were just insane but somehow passed the test.

As I ran my auto body shop doing a lot of work for my "friends," I noticed things happening around me that just flat out where not good. I remember one incident where one of my friend's associates started coming around my shop a lot.

He was a really nice guy, just as nice as anybody you or I might know. What I mean is that it was not obvious to me at the time who he was hanging out with and what he was truly about; he was clean cut, no tattoos, no tough-guy goatee, no deep New York City slang, no strange crew that he spent time with, at least not around me.

It was a Saturday morning, I remember because it was the morning after a long night at a dance club and I had a mad headache. This guy's mother was calling my shop looking for her son. She was frantic and insistent something was wrong, a mother's instinct I guess. I told her what I knew which was that I saw him about two days ago. Ends up the police found him thrown off the overpass dead on the tracks. I remember feeling bad but not so much. My attitude about it was, "Yeah, it's sad but hey things happen" and off I went working with my so-called "friends."

As the years went by more curious "things" kept happening, but at this point I was used to it. I knew it was wrong but I was isolated and I never really allowed myself to get totally out of the fog. My reality was what was closest to me and that's what I believed. It wasn't a true baseline but it was mine, so I wanted to believe it. Again, "have attitude will travel" and "play harder, be better and you'll win them over." This environment and society was perfect for that mindset.

One day I remember not hearing from my "friends" which was a little unusual so I went to their business location. When I got there it was a ghost town, NOTHING. I mean nothing PERIOD! I remembered there had been some talk around town but it wasn't good talk and I can bet they didn't relocate to a nicer location.

Now this was an opportunity for me to reflect because things were quiet and I was able look around a bit. I started to look at things differently, come out of the fog a bit and I said to myself, if I want a life like my parents' or respectable folks', I shouldn't be doing what I was doing, that was clear. Do I want this anymore? Do I want to end up relocating like my "friends"? No way!

It's funny how things work out because a major relocation did seem to fit into my life's plan perfectly right at that time but not the kind my "friends" experienced. As mentioned earlier, I was into different sports than most New York kids, I loved the beach and warm weather, so I felt that Southern California was the perfect place for me. Notice: almost the farthest geographic location from NY possible staying within the United States.

I moved to California, got serious and landed the perfect job. It was a management position for a 24/7 security firm. I made great money, no-body watched me closely and I got to be in the office on my own schedule, again the perfect cover to support my ongoing lifestyle. With a job like this I could hide in plain sight doing my thing and no one would know.

My life was going good, I bought a new car, got a pretty girl, rented a cool apartment, was working out daily and believe it or not managed to put together a little clean and sober time. Things were going really well, when about three months later I went out with some friends to a dance club. And would you believe it? A chance encounter at a club with old friends from New York inviting me to party with them had me off and running back into it all over again.

Once again I was back to "hanging out with all the wrong people, going to all the wrong places, doing all the wrong things." As I'm sure you can figure out this was a big part of the problem and later we'll talk about how it was a big part of the solution. Once we get into the fix we'll gain great clarity on this statement.

Although I continued the bottle and bag fairly frequently during my workweek, I excelled greatly working at the security company and was pro-moted to head up a new division. However, with this type of responsibility and added stress coupled with my job needing me to be more visible, it was getting harder and harder to maintain my covert bad habits.

While working for this company, I found the owner to be really dynamic, exciting and a very good businessman. We had a connection and I liked that, he was somebody I respected. Later in life I realized how much of a true mentor he really had been for me. It seemed like everything he touched worked out well. He was a very fair man to everyone but also not one to be played with. As this new division grew it required our relationship to grow and I liked that as well. As time went on I developed a lot of new excellent habits and skills.

Unfortunately for me at this point in my life I just couldn't let go of the bottle and bag stress management toolkit and this time I paid a big consequence. I was fired! Wow was I crushed and I found it very hard to get beyond it. I had let myself down and let my boss down whom I very much liked and respected and who had high hopes for me. My solution for this was... my bottle and bag stress management toolkit of course.

Flash forward through a few years of this behavior: cleaning up, landing great jobs and then finding ways to conveniently leave or find fault with the work environment and the people. Until one night in the rain I was going home from a night out at the clubs. I was wondering why it got so bright in the car all of a sudden when I came to the riveting realization that the voice I could barely hear over my pounding music was a police helicopter's civilian broadcast system phone directing me to pull over. I did so as fast as I could, and once pulled over I saw about three or four more police cars in my side-view mirrors! Oh crap!!!

As the police put me in handcuffs and searched my car I was cool as a cucumber and maintained the attitude that this would be over soon. I could smooth this out. I could get out of everything! I'd be over this minor hiccup and on with my life! But while handcuffed facedown on the grass in the rain a police officer came over to me. He bent down and if you can believe it said very calmly, "You look as if this doesn't bother you. You're acting as if you're untouchable. Let me set you straight. You seem like an intelligent nice guy but I've got news for you, you are in a world of trouble and you'd better wake up soon kid." He patted me on the shoulder and walked away.

Boy was that a wake-up call! But would I pay attention to it or continue doing what I'd always done? I was swiftly taken off to jail. Once at sentencing I remember the judge stating, "three to five years at Chino State Prison with either a parole trailer or the option." Crap!!! Yet another wake-up call! I was given a choice to do the jail time and have a conviction on my record which would make it hard to work at frigging McDonald's OR go to a court-ordered 12-step treatment program. I couldn't get out of this one without facing the music—no one could do it for me.

I might have been born recently but it wasn't yesterday. I took the treatment program option.

In chapter 2 we'll experience what my 15 years in the mainstream treatment program world was like and my results on that journey.

CHAPTER TWO

MY INTRODUCTION AND EXPERIENCE WITH THE MAINSTREAM TREATMENT PROGRAMS

·····························

I enrolled in an outpatient treatment program where I would do the requirements of the program and go home at night. At this point I was willing and did everything that I was told to the letter. I realized that I was much more than who I was displaying to the world and to myself—I was ready to make a change.

As I write this I'm closing my eyes and going back easily 17 years to my very first treatment session like it was yesterday. I remember them asking me what I thought the problem was. I drink and drug too much I said and they asked me why and so the journey begins.

The second question they asked me was to what length was I willing to go to resolve this problem? My answer was I was willing to go to any length, whatever it would take. Think about it. I was looking at several years of prison time. I had a wake-up call that rattled my cage enough for me to look at my life from several different perspectives. I was desperate to have a better life than the one I was living and knew I could do great things here on earth. I felt I was truly ready and willing to listen to anybody that made sense or no sense for that matter. I just wanted to get better. From their perspective it all started with my necessary admission that I was an alcoholic and that my life was unmanageable. While I was in the outpatient program there were several people who clearly had serious problems and there were many on occasion who portrayed acts of rebellion and violent outbursts. I was left with the clear impression that this was a common occurrence. I say this because it was plausible that my companions in the outpatient program had issues and parts of their lives were obviously unmanageable. I knew I had problems to deal with too but was I as bad off as these folks?

In treatment we mainly talked about what we were feeling and what we didn't like that was going on in our lives. We focused quite a bit on the realization that we were sick, that we had a disease and that it wasn't our fault. While in the treatment program we were introduced to AA meetings and told if we were to have any chance, the AA program and their meetings were it. Pretty much AA was the ONLY way to get clean and sober according to EVERYONE and finally the court orders you to go to AA meetings so you really aren't given much choice. Remember I was on board 100% with this plan and was willing to do whatever it would take to get better. So I didn't put up a fuss. Most of the staff at the outpatient facility were recovering alcoholics/addicts themselves and very nice people who seemed to have their lives together. So this was all the more validation and positive influence to follow the lead set before me and roll on down the AA road.

Once I finished with the six-week treatment program I was to get an AA sponsor and follow through with the 16-month court-mandated program affiliated with AA. Meaning I had to go to six regular AA meetings and one meeting at the court-mandated program a week. The court used a company that was affiliated with the national counsel for alcohol and drug abuse approved by the court system.

I was accepted into the program with open arms and made fast friends. These are very nice people and ones who would do just about

anything for you as long as you played by the AA rules. The rooms filled
a huge emotional need as well for me, feeling pretty vulnerable and confused at the time made me jump right into the family of AA and I liked all
the attention I got there.

But after 30 days I relapsed and all of a sudden I was viewed a little
differently. I noticed people didn't want to be as friendly with me anymore
while others really wanted to help. In many cases several folks wanted to
make me their pet project. At the time I was generally okay with this and
just really want to nip this in the bud.

For the first 6 months I wasn't able to get more than 30 days at
a time free from alcohol and was dubbed "Hank the relapse ranger." In
open meetings I was often the object of what not to do or who not to be.
What this did for me was confirm that I was an alcoholic and indeed my
life was unmanageable and that I was sick, really sick.

Personal belief is a funny thing. I noticed something about my drinking and drug use during this period of my newfound life of "sobriety."
My habit seemed to increase greatly and now in my mind I was more of
an alcoholic than I had ever been aware of before. This speaks to "As a
man thinketh in his heart, so he is." Now my "required" admission—that
I was an alcoholic, that my life was unmanageable and that I was sick—
was set in stone. I believed it so I became it. I resigned to the Alcoholics
Anonymous tenets and preamble which we'll talk about in greater detail
later. For now I'll mention two statements that seemed to speak to me at
the time, "Once an alcoholic, always an alcoholic" and "if you completely
give yourself to this simple program..." These told me, especially based on
my recent behavior, that I was screwed for life as far as drinking went. I
needed to follow along and do as I was told if I wanted a better life, so I
was all for it.

During the following months I went to my required six meetings a
week plus my one court-mandated class. I was able to maintain my sobriety. However something happened as I got close to my one-year mark. In
the rooms there was a lot of talk about relapse at important milestones

such as the one-year mark and to be really careful because this was where a lot of people would go out. Well I bet you can guess what happened to me? Yup, I relapsed. Bigger than ever, just as the program said I would. Again I don't feel the need to supply you with all the gory details, but trust me, my bottle and bag habits escalated along with my rogue behaviors of "have attitude will travel" and "play harder, be better and you'll win them over."

I've always been an observant person and a big student of personal development programs, such as Tony Robbins, Jack Canfield, Les Brown, Jim Rohn, etc, and something that we're taught is to be a student and not just follow the masses blindly. We are taught to be forever on the lookout for common denominators in events that happen in our lives and to look for the truth that proves or disproves the people and the path that we're following. You'll see this observation technique be quite helpful in getting to the truth and the solutions.

After my relapse I was told that this was a part of recovery. I found myself being pulled in several different directions. I was pulled by my AA sponsor, by the general population at AA meetings, by the AA gurus (that is, AA old-timers) at the meetings, by the voices inside my head.

While all this was going on one thing was for sure, my ability to stay clean and sober wasn't working the way I wanted it to. So I was willing to yet again "give myself even further to the program." I honestly don't know how much more I could have given of myself but I did anyway. This meant sometimes going to two meetings a day, more one-on-ones at coffee shops with people in AA, sponsoring people in AA yourself, constantly going to AA functions and calling at least three AA people a day just to name a few. Guess what, with this type of dedication and approach it started working. Earlier I mentioned being observant, looking for common denominators and being a student and in doing so I noticed several things.

During a meeting the program has a few selected people read at the beginning, middle and end several documents while the group listens. These documents are the preamble, the tenets and the *musts* of the program. Often these documents are read by all the people in the meeting room. Usually they are read in a monotone robotic cadence. Looking around these rooms I notice after months and years of doing this you almost look like you're in a trance-like state. Like anything else you've read, memorized or heard a million times you don't even realize what you're speaking anymore, you're just saying it. All the while little do we know that we're actually programming these words into our subconscious mind, becoming one with them.

After months of my observations more than a few things didn't add up for me but I really couldn't say much about it and chose not to. The program talks about its "impressive stats and desire not to oppose anyone," however I found out this is so far from the truth. On several occasions I and a very few others expressed our feelings or observations about some of the things that we were noticing but we were quickly chastised directly in the meetings or after the meeting by AA gurus. All the while this was supposed to be a "safe" environment to share our thoughts and feelings.

This is the room's consensus, meaning you're really only welcome if you "do as we do" and "think as we think," otherwise you'll not be welcome. Please let me say that: this is a group that I spent major time with. Within these groups I met great people and some of them would do just about anything for you. You get to know their life stories and they get to know yours. I respect all people and still have friends in the AA program.

However what happened for me was my bullshit meter started to register and things just didn't add up. I began to really look at what was going on around me, and what I saw was basically a trade from drinking and drugging to a lifestyle that was just a substitute for a normal one. This substitute took significant time and energy away from one's life, and in my opinion, most did not even come close to a balanced lifestyle. What I saw were members in zombie, robotic states, a cult status type of lifestyle. I use the word "cult" to be descriptive of a behavior type. I say this in NO way to imply that members of AA would do any harm to anybody as some in a cult may.

Let's quickly take a look at the Webster's dictionary definition of cult: A usually nonscientific method or regimen claimed by its originator to have exclusive or exceptional power in curing a particular disease.

1. A system or community of religious worship and ritual.
2. Obsessive, especially faddish, devotion to or veneration for a person, principle, or thing.

3. An instance of great veneration of a person, ideal, or thing, esp. as manifested by a body of admirers: the physical fitness cult.
4. Veneration the feeling of a person who venerates; a feeling of awe, respect, etc.; reverence: They were filled with veneration for their priests.

When we look at what the AA book says in the forward and what its members seem to push on you subtly and often not so subtly is the idea of "I hope these pages will prove so convincing that no further authentication will be necessary." Meaning they hope you wont look elsewhere.

The primary text says, "When writing or speaking publicly about alcoholism, we urge each of our Fellowship to omit his personal name... [W]e ask the press also, to observe this request, for otherwise we shall be greatly handicapped." Additionally the tenets speak of "not being able to remain a secret society."

We'll get into this cult business in greater detail later but it was pretty clear to me that they didn't want you to look anywhere else for options or solutions. It was also obvious not to bring this up in public because the "secret society" would not "live" for some reason otherwise. Hmmm... Now to me it just seems like this programming is a ploy to isolate its members. It felt very much so from where I sat, anyway.

Like I said before in the past my way of obtaining sobriety was not working, but following the program methods were. So I was compelled to not rock the boat, as opposed to asking the questions that stacked up in the back of my brain. I knew from before that questioning the AA way just did not go over well within the program.

Let's fast-forward another few years. At this time I'd achieved about five or six years of sobriety and had pulled back my attendance at meetings and involvement in the program-related activities quite a bit. My life was full of quality social activities with the world at large. Church, fitness, work, community, dating, etc... However something was missing and I still didn't know what at this point. I was catching hell from several of the program members and while being a student of life and not a follower I noticed those who were upset with me the most were the ones most immersed in the program and had the full AA "indoctrination," if you will.

For reasons I couldn't understand then, I relapsed again. Those same folks in the rooms that gave me hell for not doing as they did seemed to be almost happy that I relapsed. However there were several who were genuinely concerned for my well-being. One thing was for sure, I've never been a wallflower type of guy. I do most things in life full throttle and rogue behavior and abuse activities were no different, so those who cared had reason for concern.

After this relapse I wasn't sure I wanted to be back in the program but I knew I needed to be. I wanted to stay clean but wasn't sure how I was going to do it. A couple years went by where I was in and out of a clean and sober lifestyle. I was using the program as a solution, sometimes using church as a solution, sometimes using Tony Robbins as a solution, sometimes using my goals and dreams as a solution. But nothing was ever enough to keep me clean for long. It was extremely frustrating to say the very least.

During this time of my life I met the girl of my dreams! We had an immediate connection and she was everything I had been looking for. She was gorgeous, had a great background, very spiritual, and good natured. Her parents were quality people with strong values and had been married for forever. Her extended family really had life's greatest values in place. She always listened to me and was very supportive of my goals and dreams. When we first met we both felt like we had known each other for a long time. It was so cool and like nothing I had experienced before. I could not let this one slip between my fingers. I knew she was the one, and lucky for me she felt the same! However I knew there was a problem. I knew she was not going to have any of my antics if we were to be together. So I was left with a choice.

But as we dated I thought I was doing a good job of hiding my abuse and like anything else in the beginning I was able to, but after a while my gig was up. It's funny how things work out. After a weekend of my antics I experienced a triple whammy. I was coming back from the grocery store and hustling up three flights of stairs when suddenly I felt like I was having some kind of mild heart attack. My left arm and leg went totally numb, I felt super light-headed and my chest was killing me.

At work I was up for a promotion but was brought into my boss's office where very respectfully she told me why I was being passed over for promotion. Her words were "You're an outstanding employee and would make a great manager for this organization. However every now and again you check out mentally and it's like the lights are on but nobody's home. You get your work done but you're just not the same high performer." It was no promotion for me and man I was not happy about it!

At this point my girl (who was now my fiancée) also gave me the cold word. I had already shared with her about my issues and we were working on it together in our relationship both really wanting to be together and doing our best to make it work. But I guess for her the on-and-off Hank just wasn't cutting it anymore. I believe her words were "Hank, you are the guy for me and I love you but this thing you're doing is NOT going to work for me if we want to be together and build a family! You're going to have to make a choice." WHOAAA! That was some weekend I tell you.

After that it really wasn't a hard choice for me to make. I wasn't happy with the program, but I knew I had to do something that would work to get my life right or else I would lose everything. Since being indoctrinated into the program, I was truly lead to believe AA was the only solution if I wanted to be successful. So what else could I do? I talked myself into it saying, it isn't that bad, it can work, I'll try harder this time, besides the people are very nice.

So again I got back involved in the traditional program, however this time it was different. Fast-forward a bit now. Happily married with one kid and another on the way I found a strong desire to act in ways that matched my values. This meant being far more balanced in my life; my physical health and fitness, the social aspects of my life outside of AA, my contribution to the world, my family life, my church life, my career, my hobbies, my finances, etc...

I was attending only about two or three meetings a week which at first I received all kinds of flack for from people in the rooms. However after a while for the most part they left me alone. I believe the contributing factors to desiring only a few meetings a week were that my life was shaping up to be a pretty cool one and I was living a balanced life outside the program. My family and I were rolling along just fine and I didn't feel the need or have the desire to be at the meetings all that much.

After our second son was born we relocated back east where both our extended families lived so we could raise our kids closer to them. I got involved in the program in the area where we lived and life kept rolling along. But after about two years unfortunately my father, the greatest man I knew, died from cancer and it sent me into a downhill spiral. Of course the well-meaning suggestions in the rooms were to go to more meetings, get deeper involved in the program, etc, but it was no use. Needless to say I relapsed again at this point back into the bottle.

If I were reading this I'd probably be saying, what the hell is up with this guy? He needs to seriously try something different! ...Yah think?! During all these relapses the gurus in the program and the general instruction from scores of people in the meetings varied. However the main message was you're not working the program hard enough, you didn't do the 12 steps thoroughly enough; maybe you're not done yet; you need to go to more meetings or you need to change your sponsor... Frankly, it wasn't easy to find any alternative for staying clean and sober and I didn't know where else to turn. I felt buried alive by the AA way and I was crying out for anything to help!

I really did give it everything I had and then some. I would hope that this was evident by the many things that I had done right in life. My life was much more than a man struggling to stay clean and sober falling off the wagon again and again.

- I owned numerous successful businesses.
- I became a high performance complex rate pilot and achieved a master's degree in the combat martial arts.
- I invented training tools and created training systems for the United States government, which is "responsible for saving thousands of U.S. lives." (United States Military quote.)
- I published several articles in top industry publications.
- And at the time of this writing, I've been happily married for well over 10 years and have five beautiful kids.

I say all this not to impress you but to impress upon you that when I set my sights on something I get it done, at least in most areas of my life. Hopefully some of these accolades are an example of this type of thorough effort AA talks about. So what was missing? Why couldn't I get this? Why was my sobriety proving over and over again to be so elusive? It must be something, but what?

There is a reason why, and within the next few chapters we're going to reveal it. We will find out what I and thousands of people have done to overcome their issues without having to become part of a secret society, without having to go to five, seven or 10 meetings a week. Without having a sponsor telling you what to do and who to do it with and without having to believe some trumped-up lie that you're powerless and have a disease.

I think you'll agree that I've exhausted all efforts using this approach; I believe I clearly qualify as a person who at the time had a substantial bottle and bag abuse issue or habit. So please stay with me as I transition from a seemingly hopeless case to a victor who found out he never had a disease. That he was only doomed because he believed he was doomed and who found a way to move from the bad tracks to the good tracks with just one lane change. Yes, one lane change! You or the person you're reading this for can do the same thing once armed with the truth. I promise you it will make your quest light-years easier!

It was at this point I started to seriously look to other places for solu-

tions and in life the best things are hard to find. I found this to be very true. You must search, dream, try, persevere, get back up when you fall down, try the next idea on the list when the 1,000th idea fails. Get my point? But most people are not willing to face that truth, they want easy street.

I started looking at all the different programs out there, talking with people going to church recovery programs, seeing a therapist, talking to the dog, talking with God, looking on the Internet. On occasion still going to meetings thinking maybe the folks in the meetings are right and I'm just an idiot. Maybe I need to give it another shot. Thank God I kept a student's mentality on the forefront and maintained a forever observant eye.

As I looked around the meetings I would sometimes attend I remember feeling sad. Feeling sad that I wasn't living the full and complete life I knew I could and that my friends in the meetings were also not living their lives to a level that they could. Here's the kicker, what I saw were people who were sold a bag of goods and believed this was the best they could do. They were sold the lie, hook, line and sinker. I guess for some that's okay. But it wasn't for me and it's not what I wish for others.

This was the start of my journey to get it right. I became the lonesome cowboy on my horse searching, damn determined to find it, whatever that was, and get the life I knew was out there.

During the next few stubborn years I stayed clean and sober doing a blend of things. As I mentioned earlier I tried traditional treatment/meetings, church-related things, L. Ron Hubbard, therapy, Tony Robbins and personal development stuff, some flat-out pure desire to be better stuff, etc... I was open to all resources in hopes that I would find something that would hit the spot, resonate and stick. Guess what?... I found it.

As a senior-level combat instructor serving the military, law enforcement and the high-risk operator community, I teach that the first task in training is "fact finding." This is the very important task of finding out how skilled the student is in all areas of combat under pressure situations. Once this drill is completed everybody plus the student knows just how much skill he or she has. For the moment their alpha ego defense system has been brought down and we have a student that is reasonable and open to learning based on the facts in front of him. He or she is able to see the truth that was there all the time. This is usually a WOW moment for the student.

We'll now uncover my WOW moments and truths that were revealed to me during my quest for a life free from drugs and alcohol and the AA way.

Then we get to fixin' this mess.

CHAPTER THREE

BLOWING THE WHISTLE ON THE FOUNDATION THAT THE MAINSTREAM TREATMENT INDUSTRY SITS ON!

....

A s we move forward into these next few chapters we will reference several different resources of study and current medical
research by some of the best doctors on the topic of alcohol
and drug abuse and my observations as an individual within the treatment culture for over 17 years.

Before we launch into this chapter I would like to ask you to be patient and stay with me as these next three chapters are the meat and po-
tatoes of my research and reveal the lies we've bought over the years. But
to achieve this I had to read dozens of books and countless medical and
industry journals, written in medical/technical terminology, after reading
three pages of which you would likely need to take a nap.

I've done my best to convey what I found in an easy read style, however in order for you to see what I want you to see there is just no way
around providing some of the medical and technical content and speak...

...After a while when I sat in treatment, meetings or one-on-one sit-downs, I started asking myself these questions: "Ok, says who? What evidence do you have for me? Prove it! I really don't see the recovery you're talking about happening for people in the rooms and it definitely isn't happening for me."

As I started questioning the mainstream treatment methods and behaviors of people in or out of treatment culture and society, it was my research that confirmed my thoughts and observations.

I now believe the term "disease" has been grossly misused in connection with alcoholism and addiction as well as many other life issues. There are syndromes or diseases popping up right and left these days if you ever watch TV. So whatever alcoholism or addiction is, it's left to be self- or coercion diagnosed but not expected to be medically treated. If you had a suspicion that you might have a medical disease of some type wouldn't your first instinct be to search out a doctor or physician and get help? Hey that's what you're supposed to do if you have restless leg syndrome!

My business mentors always taught me to ask a very important question when new information was attained. What evidence do I have that has drawn me to my conclusions or assumptions?

So I ask you the same, where did your knowledge and confirmation of the disease of alcoholism come from? What evidence do you have to support your assumption? Was it derived from the idea that it just is? An alternative point of view is never closely looked at and this way of thinking is just accepted or an applied assumption. We think if the doctors are calling it a disease it must really be one. Have you known someone that actually was ordered by a doctor to take a blood test and was then found to have the cells that signal the disease of alcoholism?

Ok another question: What disease doesn't show up in a body dead or living, is self-diagnosed and is fixed spiritually by nonmedical personnel?

Hmmm... Sounds like some voodoo, black magic, dark knight stuff to me.

Let's take a look at the pieces of my sarcastic yet truthful question.

The answer is: the disease of alcoholism and drug addiction based on our general society and mainstream treatment centers. Most in the medical society, insurance companies and treatment centers will tell us we as alcoholics have a "medical disease." That this disease is characterized by self-destructiveness, compulsion, loss of control, and a mysterious, as-yet-unidentified physiological component and the best solution is... treatment which basically goes hand in hand with the AA program.

Most of the media depict addiction as a condition where the addict, no matter what, cannot control his/her behavior. So therefore the loss of control or lack of choice in the matter must equate to a disease. Why would anyone choose on their own to act in the outrageous ways some addicts do, impossible, right? We now know that there are many levels of addiction and it varies as much as there are individual experiences and personalities in the world. And the media has taught us to think if we have no control over use of drugs and alcohol it must be a "medical disease." This is highly misguided and an extremely limited concept. But this idea of a loss of control leading to a "disease" became the cornerstone for the modern disease concept.

What about a disease of the mind? Well if you ask me I would say how does that idea account for the 75% of society who got better all on their own? Did they just wake up one day and miraculously become disease-free? Jeffrey Schaler, PhD, called this very convenient phenomenon a "spontaneous remission" in his book *Addiction Is a Choice.* It is not a disease or "allergy" of the mind. The seed that is planted and grown in the mainstream treatment industry is one that is nurtured by a false self-concept of weakness and lack of control, so therefore the person is coerced or gives in to the idea that he has a diseased mind and body with no hope for recovery unless he completely gives himself over to the culture. And all of this cultivation, with absolutely no evidence or true facts to back up what is being preached, therefore keeps the "diseased" sick for good.

So if the disease model has the belief that it's of the body (physiological) and the brain (psychological), this concept becomes a mind game that can have a huge influence over whether a person will become an alcoholic or a drug addict and another will not. An addict is drenched in thoughts such as, You have a disease, you're sick, you're powerless, the disease is always doing push-ups, watch out for milestones such as the first month or first year, the disease is cunning and baffling, etc. These turn into a self-fulfilling prophecies and when coupled with the fact that treatment programs teach you that you do not have the power to moderate your consumption this is where the self-fulfilling prophecy kicks into high gear and then you prove the limiting source right!

In Dr. Schaler's book, *Addiction Is a Choice*, he defines diseases as "medical conditions. They can be discovered on the basis of bodily signs [not behavior]. They are something people have. They are involuntary." A simple yet reliable way to test for a true physical disease is whether it can be shown to exist in a corpse. Again according to Dr. Schaler's book, "There are no bodily signs of addiction...that can be identified in a dead body." Furthermore pathologists use standard pathology textbooks which have all the classification of diseases. And guess what, alcohol and addiction are not listed within these books.

When I found this definition in Dr. Schaler's research with John Hopkins University it blew me away. Think about it, any real disease that I've ever heard of can be found in an autopsy. Things such cancer, Parkinson's disease, diabetes, heart disease or a tumor can be seen in the body's tissue.

Let's be clear here: The effects of alcohol and drugs can be found in the body tissue. The abuse of drugs and alcohol can cause other diseases to become present such as liver disease or cancer. But back to the pathologist textbook: "no such identifiable pathology has been found in the bodies of heavy drinkers and drug users except for the fact that if you drink too much you stress your body and can cause a break down of proper functions which can lead to many physical problems with your health."

Check out for yourself at one of the many resources online or search for other online pathology textbooks. If you look close you don't see alcoholism or addiction listed at all!

So if it doesn't fit under a physical or mental disease where does it go?

Additionally alcoholism and addiction are not listed in the *American Psychiatric Association's Diagnostic and Statistical Manual of Mental Disorders IV* (DSM-IV) -TR.

What was once listed in the this manual as alcoholism is now referred to as alcohol dependence and abuse. These are listed under the category of substance-related disorders.

This is very similar to the once-held belief and classification by the medical profession that homosexuality was a disease; this was declassified in 1973 and is now classified as a nondisease.

In this excerpt from the National Institute of Alcohol Abuse and Alcoholism website, the idea of alcoholism as a disease is not even mentioned:

"What are symptoms of an alcohol use disorder?

"A few mild symptoms—which you might not see as trouble signs—can signal the start of a drinking problem. It helps to know the signs so you can make a change early. If heavy drinking continues, then over time, the number and severity of symptoms can grow and add up to an "alcohol use disorder." Doctors diagnose an alcohol use disorder, generally known as alcohol abuse or alcoholism, when a patient's drinking causes distress or harm. See if you recognize any of these symptoms in yourself. And don't worry—even if you have symptoms, you can take steps to reduce your risks."

Let's take a look at some more quotes from other professionals and what they had to say about the disease label.

"Generally in this chapter I have avoided using the term 'alcoholism,' for although the word communicates meaning given the extent to which the concept described issues regarding alcohol use and abuse the deserved attention in this chapter and I will broach these subsequently. I will not however become enmeshed in specific definitional issues related to what I regard as the inadequately validated construct of alcoholism."

"In reviewing the history of the concept of alcoholism, Paredes (1976) has noted that the problems we label "alcoholism" have been conceptualized variously throughout history as an expression of the free will of individuals, the result of transcendental influences on the person, psychological responses to experiential stress, an epiphenomenon of disturbances in the social system, a disease, and a learned behavior." **Above excerpts taken from** ***Medical and Social Aspects of Alcohol Abuse***, **by Boris Taba-koff, Patricia B. Sutker, and Carrie L. Randall**

. . . .

"In recent Years, 'addiction' has become an extremely popular term for describing a wide range of behaviors formerly called 'sins.'

"Many would agree that defining sin is best left to religious communities, but the convergence of religion and science in the 12-step recovery movement has brought us full circle to a most pernicious mind trap called 'addictive disease.' This expression, which means the disease of sin, is a subtle fusion of opposite meaning that can go unnoticed by even sophisticated intellects.

"Like a faulty rivet that sends the ship to the bottom of the sea, the disease concept of addiction is the fatal flaw in our addiction care system. The 'sin' of intemperance has been misidentified as disease, calling forth a practice called 'treatment,' which, if understood as 'exorcism,' might well be suited for combating sin, but which is only marginally useful in the treatment of disease." - ***Rational Recovery***, **by Jack Trimpey**

. . . .

"Once we realize that addiction cannot be classified as a literal disease, its nature as an ethical choice becomes clearer. A person starts, moderates or stops drinking because that person wants to! People do the same thing with drugs and tobacco. Such choices reflect the person's values. The person chooses to use drugs or refrains from using drugs because he or she finds meaning in doing so!" - Addiction Is a Choice, by Dr. Schaler

. . . .

"I accept that 12-step supporters are completely devoted to the 12-step philosophy. When something appears to have saved you (or others), loyalty is natural. What I don't accept willingly is anyone being told that the 12-steps are the only way to overcome addiction...In reality there are many ways to overcome addiction. AA is one of them but it is not the only one. Saying otherwise is potentially a disastrous disservice to some individuals. I hope that this disservice fades away quickly." - Sex, Drugs, Gambling & Chocolate, by Dr. A. Thomas Horvath

Within the Big Book's 12 steps God is mentioned eight times and part of the AA credo statement is that you must "give yourself over to this simple program" which includes "doing" or "working" the 12 steps. This is what is necessary to have your "spiritual awakening" or to remove the "sin" as in Jack Trimpey's statement about exorcism.

Today any socially unacceptable behavior is likely to be diagnosed or described metaphorically as a disease or addiction. However this metaphorical term has been taken literally and all these new "isms" and addictions are claimed to be medical diseases.

Based on much of the latest research alcohol disorder boils down to this: a behavior challenge which classifies the person as an "alcoholic" or an "addict" based on their behavioral actions. And according to Dr.

Horvath these behavioral actions can "label" the person as such by way of the "three C's"—cravings, consequence and loss of control—in accordance to the traditional definition of disease. Dr. Horvath also says that this is highly contradictive as we now understand that there is a huge range of addiction out there. You wouldn't say I have a disease if I am addicted to working out or reading books or attending yard sales. There isn't any definitive place or line to draw where addiction begins for someone but we know that it is tied greatly to our emotions. Our emotions drive our actions and our actions are our intentional conduct, meaning how we choose to portray ourselves to the world. Back to referencing Dr. Schaler's awesome quote, a person can choose to start or stop drugs and alcohol because they find meaning in doing just that! I believe it is always a personal choice no matter what!

Question: What disease is self-diagnosed or admitted to through coercion?

If you have a disease you should be able to go to the doctor and he or she should be able to run some tests and say okay we found it, right? Remember we're looking for proof that a disease exists, not the effects or results from bad habits/actions.

This brings us to the disease of hammeritis. Please allow me to tell you my simple, humorous and hopefully pertinent story that demonstrates hammeritis for you and the dents in my cousin's neighbor's head and kneecaps.

My cousin Delbert's neighbor is severely inconsiderate and continues to park his beat-up two-tone Cadillac (which takes up two spots) in front of Delbert's house after politely being asked to stop more than once.

He did this even with the knowledge that my cousin's wife was pregnant with twins and if she couldn't get a spot in front of her own home she would have to walk a few blocks back in the dead of winter, this doesn't stop him.

Well this goes on for months. Then one unfortunate winter evening Delbert's wife parks her car two blocks down and walks home because her spot was—you guessed it—being used by this lovely neighbor's ugly car.

As luck may have it this particular evening she slips on some ice and goes into premature labor.

My cousin and his wife spend days at the hospital and she's put on bed rest for the rest of her pregnancy. Five days later on their way home Delbert runs into this "favorite" neighbor of theirs at the local home improvement store. As the two of them are having a spirited discussion about what happened that night, this neighbor says to Delbert, "Man I'm sorry but you should have gotten a closer parking spot!"

Well that was it! Delbert loses it, grabs the nearest hammer, whacks his neighbor in the kneecap and bops him on the head.

Okay, so from this simple and stupid story you may say, so what I don't get it. Well let's ask a question; what made cousin Delbert react that way? Back to the story, In Delbert's world the experts in the mainstream medical profession say he has a disease called hammeritis, which is characterized by self-destructiveness, compulsive behavior, loss of control and some mysterious, as-yet-unidentified physiological component.

Oh, he has a disease everyone says! Well okay, everybody can understand his actions then and he gets a pass... Seriously though in the real world would he get a pass on his behavior even though we all could logically understand why he did it? No, he wouldn't! Delbert would have to pay a consequence for his actions no matter what. That's right—so why is it okay for the alcoholic disease model to not take responsibility? I know AA-ers are not running around bopping people on the head and kneecaps claiming their disease of hammeritis is to blame but we keep hearing that alcoholics should not be held accountable for their actions because these are the outpourings of a "sick brain," that they are sick, unable to think rationally and incapable of giving up alcohol by themselves!

Can you see my point for the mainstream treatment disease idea? It's a huge cop-out to yourself and to your society using this disease concept to handle your addiction!

Those who created this self-diagnosed disease idea say, "If you feel addicted, you're addicted." Okay, but what about the opposite statement,

"I don't feel addicted so I'm not addicted." Logically that statement must be true too. I bet those who created this thought would feel different if I said that to them over and over or if they spoke it to themselves. But in mainstream if you say "no" to their ideas then you're in the "denial phase" according to 97% of the mainstream treatment industry. There is just no wiggle room at all for free thinking.

What kind of nonsense is this? To me it's just ridiculous! How about this: "If you feel diabetic, you are diabetic" or "If you feel like you have hammeritis, you have hammeritis" and so therefore you shouldn't be held accountable for your actions. I can't believe people actually believe this!

The second part of our question is the use of coercion to admit that you have a disease. If you were not aware of this, a part of the disease model credo is, "Most alcoholics don't know they have a problem and must be forced to recognize they are alcoholics and addicts," writes Dr. Schaler *(Addiction Is a Choice*, p. 4).

For me, the problem with the use of coercion was not admitting that I had a problem. That was clear to me. It was the admission of this disease idea... We'll talk more about this later but for starters in AA admitting you are powerless and that 12-step treatment is the only solution is a huge part of it. Well let me say it again—75% of people with drinking and drug problems stop on their very own!!! That's an enormous percentage! I was blown away when I learned this!!!

In one study done by Harvard Medical School headed up by George Vaillant, MD, who also happens to be on the Board of Trustees of AA, found that at least 60% of alcoholics who achieved five years or more of clean time did it without the help of AA.

Something I found that was consistent with my observations over the years and I'm sure you'll find as mind-blowing as I did was that the AA drop rate is unbelievably high.

The following chart was created from a five-year internal study done by AA. Why is it that we're led to believe different? Why is it that they don't make this data as easily found as the idea that we have a disease

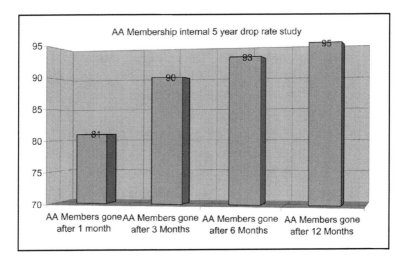

AA Membership internal 5 year drop rate study

and need a spiritual makeover?

Other studies done at the National Institute on Alcohol Abuse and Alcoholism state that 75% of alcoholics freed themselves without the use of a treatment program.

What would you call that, "spontaneous remission"? I call it making smarter choices.

I never felt that I was powerless and I don't believe that I am. Walking around with this mindset only reinforced the idea that I was supposedly powerless which can dangerously and so easily equate to... why even try, I'm powerless anyway... Sounds like a disease called excusitis to me.

Let me tell you what; I was given so much crap about my ways of thinking by so many of the hard-core AA folks. I was basically shunned by them and told "see, you're in denial!" and that this "denial" was a major symptom of the disease. This in turn made many other folks in the rooms leery of me. I can personally tell you it does not make you feel very warm and welcome in there at all having all those vibes coming at you. This was one of the more subtle forms of coercion.

Let's talk about some of the more outright blatant acts of coercion and conversion using denial tactics.

"Several years ago two college students were arrested for bringing marijuana into the U.S. from Jamaica. Although they smoked pot occasionally, their main motive in bringing it in was to make money.

"After a month in jail and numerous hearings, they were ordered into treatment. A few years later, one of the students was getting straight A's and was now looking to get into law school. The two had been ordered into multiple and weekly meetings for therapy and 12-step group meetings for many months.

"At one point one of the students told a therapist that he'd brought the drugs into the country to make money, which he needed for school and other expenses, and that having to attend all these therapy and 12-step sessions was getting in the way of his school studies.

"The therapist replied that it didn't matter whether he failed college. The important thing for the therapist was that he was being treated for his disease. Any disagreement with the therapist or with the 12-step religion was labeled 'denial,' a symptom of the disease. Eventually, this student went along (coerced) with the nonsense, and was released from treatment."
    - *Addiction is a Choice,* by Dr. Schaler

"A man convinced against his will is of the same opinion still."

In many mainstream treatment centers this situation has gotten out of control. The denial issue affects so many people who really want help but if they don't admit to all of the disease model criteria they are denied service from insurance companies, shunned and looked down upon by people in the mainstream society and made to feel extremely isolated, confused and alone. I've been a witness to this firsthand.

Answer to: What disease is self-diagnosed or admitted to through coercion? I say, none!!!

This is the ideal spot to introduce the first of the 5 keys of the 5 master key formula. We will use this key to unlock the things that are holding you back.

The first key is:

True perspective knowledge (TPK)

The perspective that you have puts a filter on the way you look at and deal with things in life. Your perspectives and perceptions are strongly held beliefs and rules that can sometimes blind you to new solutions. When we resist new ideas we reject new ways of thinking before we even give them a chance. This is why we must gain a new or fresh view based on "true perspective knowledge." This idea of true perspective knowledge is essentially what the first portion of the book is all about: having a new and clearer vision. This is so important in gaining your freedom. If you can't get this key then don't even bother with the rest. In the second portion of the book we will teach you how to use all of these 5 keys.

Let me take you back to a section of our first question: What disease is fixed spiritually by nonmedical personnel?

Think about this for a second. If you have a disease like cancer, Parkinson's, diabetes, heart disease or a tumor would you trust your health to someone who has no medical knowledge but gave you instruction based on his own experience and what he or she thought was best for you? This is exactly what happens in the mainstream treatment programs and has been going on for decades! To add to the insanity this "fix it" person (therapist, treatment center, sponsor, etc) uses a one size fits all faith healing approach to remedy the problem. It's like bringing your Porsche, Maserati or Austin Martin to the local mechanic and trusting him to use the Big

Book of Automotive Repair to successfully fix a specifically precision en-
gineered piece of machinery valued at 10 to 25 times the amount of the
average automobile. Forget the value of the fact that the mechanic simply
does not know the machine and hasn't been properly trained in fixing it!
This is just a simple example I've used to try to paint a picture for you. But
we are not really talking about your car are we? We're talking about YOU
and your LIFE!!!

I'm fairly confident that you would agree that if your mom or dad
had brain cancer you would not be comfortable with a first year intern
performing the brain surgery, right? Right!

Let me reiterate to you that this type of thing happens every day
in the mainstream treatment world. People who have only strung together
less than a year can become your sponsor, as well as counselors in the
industry who only have a few years under their belt and are not armed
with all the true facts. And on top of this they're mostly using Bob's Big
Book of Auto Mechanics to fix unique individuals and complex problems
shoving them through the same box regardless of their individualities.

Consider this idea... "While I live my life I have to live with myself
and at the end of my life I will ask, Did I like the life that I lived?"

It is my charge to you that you will not be limited by anything or
anyone, that you will not fall into the lethal traps of unqualified others
who want to control and shape your life but for you to be given all the
current, correct tools and resources to thrive and live out your potential
to the fullest. All of us are capable of achieving outstanding lives, however to realize this our minds cannot be filled with self-limiting thoughts.
Thoughts that tell us we're defective, diseased, out of control and under
the control of an obscured, destructive and unproven entity. Think enough
of yourself to at least do your own homework and find out the truth. Remember the proper diagnosis is half the cure, and the other half has been
done by millions of people before you and me. It is all possible! This is
outlined for you in part 2.

So my reality was that I was not truthfully informed. Don't waste years like I did. Please read on to find out more truth and I hope you'll stick with me all the way to the end and get yourself that freedom we all deserve!

Answer to: What disease is fixed spiritually by nonmedical personnel? None.

After I was armed with the truth I was mad as hell.

I've found out that most people who are in recovery don't know about any of these truths and once they're told they act like deer in headlights! They don't know what to do or say and then something happens...

You can sit and watch them go into shutdown mode as if a parent has just been told their child has been caught stealing, doing drugs or having sex. You can see their mind racing "You must have my child mixed up with some other kid. My child would never do such a thing, it can't be true."

They usually refuse to believe it and the topic changes very quickly or they either have to fix the radiator leak in the 57 Chevy that they don't have or they conveniently have to take the meat loaf out of the oven... or they get VERY mad. Try it!

Now that we've blown the whistle on the medical disease idea, pulled the covers on if it is a disease and discovered how self- or coercion diagnosis is not plausible and even dangerous, can you see how we have been misguided and mislead? Or can you at least look at what we've been sold here as possibly questionable? Do you know who in their right mind would follow the lead of a nonmedical "expert" for a solution to a truly fatal disease? No one! Therefore how can this disease concept be true at all! Flat out, we've been lied to.

Did you know that the reason alcoholism and addiction was labeled a disease primarily was so that hospitals and medical insurance companies could then charge for their services? People I'm talking about an approach to healing that is decades old and based on greed! Think about how much we as humans have grown in the last 20 years alone, all the medical knowledge and science exploration that has been uncovered so how can we keep going on this outdated and I believe harmful way to health.

Earlier in the chapter I mentioned that the disease label inserted in the professional treatment industry funds their very existence. What do I mean with this statement? Who would have the most to gain from what is now a $100 billion industry? It is asking these questions that helps bring clarity to why in 1954 it was a major win for the American Medical Association to accept abusive drinking as a "disease."

First let's take a look at a few things that make much more sense to me in how alcohol, drug abuse and most any other immediate gratification habit could possibly develop and become a majorly destructive problem in our lives.

In our culture and around the world we see alcohol as a socially accepted lubricant. It may be socially accepted but let's make no mistake about it, it is a drug! It's important to add that it is one of the oldest recreational drugs out there. Alcohol is the drug ethanol which is a volatile, toxic, flammable and colorless liquid.

It's more than just a drink. It's more than just, let's have a few at happy hour. It's more than just a nightcap. This is a powerful psychoactive drug, PERIOD. You can run a combustion engine off this stuff!

This psychoactive drug is in the same category as psycho pharmaceutical or psychotropic sub-stances. Other drugs that fall into this category are marijuana, heroin, antidepressants, cocaine, crack, hash and methamphetamines just to name a few.

These drugs affect the central nervous system; change our metabolism; attack the liver, joints, stomach, pancreas, and blood and alter brain function, impacting the perception management center which affects consciousness, mood, cognition and behavior.

For a drug to be psychoactive it must cross the blood-brain barrier affecting the neurochemical function. With long-term use and in many cases even a one-time exposure, psychoactive substances can change the structure and function of neurons. This is where in your brain the whole "addiction thing" happens!

Okay. Let's get right down to it... We cannot expect to take a drug over a long period of time and not have anything happen to the body and the brain. There is no way a drug that passes the blood-brain barrier will not reek havoc on the central nervous system (which controls behaviors, senses, movement skills, voluntary and involuntary functions of the body), change the perception management center (how we perceive events in our lives) and saturate the liver. All this only to have a nonmedical person prescribe a fix. More importantly without focusing on a person's nutritional, brain and bodily needs how can we expect a real complete change to occur?

To put this in an additional perspective to understand how easily and deceptively harmless this disease model and the learned helplessness problem can take root we begin looking at when someone is young. They start with seeing Mom and Dad having drinks with friends or watching Dad enjoy his beer with a football game. Mom opens up a bottle of wine when her sister comes over to talk. At holidays the wine is flowing and the special bottle of whisky is opened up to enjoy.

All the while over the years television commercials, billboard ads, hospitals, churches and schools have promoted literature claiming that if you see a friend, parent or classmate with XYZ behaviors they're sick and may a have a disease.

This goes on into the late teens and young adulthood. Now we get into going out with friends for drinks on Friday night, beers at the barbeque or glass of wine or two with the girls after dropping off the kids.

This transitions into:

- To have a good time, drink or drug.
- To make a bad time better, drink or drug.
- To make a good time better, drink or drug.
- Go out for drinks and a good time at happy hour on Wednesday after work—drink or drug.
- Go out for happy hour Friday after work—drink or drug.
- After a spirited fight with the husband or wife, have of smoke of whatever to level off your mood.

■ Work is stressful—have a drink to level off your mood.

■ You're going to a backyard party an hour away from home, after stressing on the ride with the kids in the car and to help deal with them at the party—have a few drinks.

This gymnastic routine goes on for years, then decades, and as time goes on your tolerance to these drugs gets higher and your body and mind have gotten saturated like a filter that doesn't filter any more—you are pickled!

It shouldn't be a stretch to see that this kind of screwing with the body's major organs changes the structure of the brains neuro connections, making direct mental associations with, "problem—have a drink," "want good time—have a drink," "want better time—have another drink." Over decades it's going to have a huge effect on the body and cause major issues that must be fixed! And they must be fixed by focusing on them specifically. They will not magically get better.

This is basic stuff, yes or no? Then why is it that mainstream treatment facilities do very little or in most cases nothing to focus on the mind and body repair using tools that are available to us every day and are proven to make a dramatic difference in a very little amount of time.

You as a recovering person can get further faster with much less effort by applying your own common sense with a little of the right information. The correct applied information can be the key to a better life for you or your loved one. Remember we are in the information age, meaning the very information at our fingertips is getting us further faster as a human race.

As we move forward let's get some more education on the fact that the treatment programs' foundation is built on one big lie and that they rarely work, often make it harder for people to "recover" and are detrimental to a truly better balanced quality of life. In addition somebody is financially making out big time here... Let's find out who.

CHAPTER FOUR

MORE IRREFUTABLE EVIDENCE TO BREAK ANY DOUBTS THAT WE'VE BEEN LIED TO

· ·

Okay, let's dig in. Some 97% of mainstream treatment uses Alcoholics Anonymous and the 12-step approach for a means of recovery. As we move forward we will break this down and fit these additional pieces into the puzzle that we're putting together.

In the beginning I didn't question anything I just wanted to focus on my recovery. Even though I saw all these lies going on around me I looked past them as do many members of the treatment culture.

In the rooms the indoctrination of the program into the mindset and one's personal admission of weakness/powerlessness coupled with a belief that we are not like others (they call nonaddicts "normies" in AA) is really essential to a person's success according to this mainstream treatment program culture.

While I sit in front of my computer I'm experiencing a semi queasy feeling remembering and seeing from my perspective now what was happening to me then. For me my experience started out not bad, but again I was ready to listen and believe whatever I was told. Initially it all made sense to me the way it was laid out. Once the program staff was convinced that I believed I was totally screwed up, that my ideas, beliefs and thinking were spiritually bankrupt and that I was powerless unless I put my trust in a power greater than myself, I was cleared to move on. At this point in the beginning I was Okayed to go to AA meetings and gain a sponsor relationship with frequent check-ins at the outpatient facility. I felt good that I was working on myself and my sobriety. Back then it felt like I was headed in the right direction. It felt harmless. And I suppose it would have been if it were all based on truth. Let's look at the Alcoholics Anonymous preamble.

This is what is read at the beginning of most meetings and what the program foundation sits on. The preamble reads as follows:

> "Alcoholics Anonymous is a fellowship of men and women who share their experience, strength and hope with each other that they may solve their common problem and help others to recover from alcoholism. The only requirement for membership is a desire to stop drinking. There are no dues or fees for AA membership; we are self-supporting through our own contributions. AA is not allied with any sect, denomination, politics, organization or institution; does not wish to engage in any controversy, neither endorses nor opposes any causes. Our primary purpose is to stay sober and help other alcoholics to achieve sobriety."

> - © by the AA Grapevine, Inc

I want to break this down for you, so let's take a good hard look and start with **"The only requirement for membership is a desire to stop drinking."** Let's say you're not sure if you have a drinking problem and you want to test the waters of AA or you just don't buy the disease concept but need help. At the beginning of a meeting or as meetings progress sometimes people are called on to read or share. The standard or accepted answer to being called on or before a share is "Hi I'm Joe and I'm an alcoholic, a drunk, an addict, etc..." But if you were to say "Hi my name is Joe and I used to have a drinking problem," forget it! The group usually responds with boos, hisses and the like. I experienced this personally.

Did you know that the words "I am" spoken to oneself are the most powerful words in personal mental programming and belief development? Think about it for a moment. If you think/speak to yourself over and over "I am a good person," your subconscious responds to it and makes it so. The same is true if you think/speak "I am a bad person" or "I am fat, smart, strong, confused, worthy, doomed, etc." Your subconscious is so much more powerful than you know. I would guess that most people don't even consider their subconscious on even the smallest level and this is very dangerous. We must be so careful with what we choose to download onto our "computer" of the mind—we are responsible for programming ourselves and our beliefs about ourselves. So if this is true, why on earth would someone consistently describe themselves by saying, "I am an alcoholic"? Or "I am powerless"? These statements are not empowering whatsoever. In fact they are just the opposite! I believe this could be one of the major contributing factors to the documented 5% success ratio of mainstream treatment programs.

Aside from the boos and hisses, reactions to those who eliminate the "I am" statement during introductions have included being spoken to after the meeting by group elders about the dangers of such talk and being told this type of talk is bad for new members, who may get the wrong idea. I've personally received phone calls saying that I'm probably different and that my martial arts and military discipline has aided me. That I'm to remember the disease is always doing push-ups, just waiting for me to mess up, and bam you're off and running back to the bar.

Needless to say this did not make me feel truly accepted at all! But my choices were to succumb to their wishes or be the brunt of their jokes. I kept going.

Moving on through the AA preamble, let's look at **"The only require-**

ment for membership is a desire to stop drinking." Well...that is not really true. It's much more like you must "do as we do," "say as we say," and "think as we think." "Oh and by the way if you don't you're not really welcome." Hmmm...to me that sounds slightly cultish, don't you think?

"There are no dues or fees for AA membership; we are self-supporting through or own contributions." Sounds dignified, however this is another incomplete truth. At some point during the meeting a collection plate is passed around the room and everyone is expected to give at a level often set by the group's "servants" (this is the title that AA uses for its leaders or meeting place workers). I do believe this is reasonable for a group to self-sustain its place of meeting. However money is not the only form of payment. Once involved in the "secret society," requests are constantly placed on your time. You'll often hear terms like "the meeting before the meeting," "the meeting after the meeting," "one-on-one meetings," "AA comes before everything else," "whatever you put in front of AA you will lose" and the list goes on. From personal experience and in numerous endless conversations with others, their own family members and friends often become alienated and although they are invited to gatherings most do not feel welcome at all in this "secret society." Why? Because it's just that—a secret society, where "normies" (AA lingo for people who don't have a drinking problem) just don't understand, don't get it and never will. This assault on your pocketbook of time has had dire outcomes for the families of AA members. When members are putting their meetings and AA friends' needs before their own family's, children's and spouse's needs they fall into a dangerous trap. I have personally seen and experienced jealousy, suspicion, isolation, neglect and broken trust just to name a few within families who take the AA commitment to an extreme.

Going back over "self-supporting through our own contributions," the AA organization has been known to take large sums of money from various cities to bring conventions to their area so the participants will spend money within that city. AA makes tens of millions on its affiliate relationships with treatment centers for its books and literature. So where does all that money go? Let's explore the next section to answer that.

"AA is not allied with any sect, denomination, politics, organization or institution; does not wish to engage in any controversy, neither endorses nor opposes any causes."

First let's look at "not being allied with politics, organizations or institutions." This statement should read more like "what sect, denomination, politics, organization or institution isn't AA involved with?"

The National Council on Alcoholism and Drug Dependence (NCADD), which in my opinion is the front for AA, requests annual dues from its affiliation groups. They were the driving force behind AA during its early years.

Marty Mann was the first woman in AA and the founder of the NCADD who employed both Bill Wilson and Dr. Bob Smith, the founders of AA. Mann's dream was to educate the whole world about the disease of alcoholism.

The following is taken directly from the NCADD website and clearly illustrates the political relationship building blocks.

"In the mid to late 1960's the federal government and President Johnson appointed Marty Mann to the national advisory commission on alcoholism providing seed money for the multiple states alcoholism effort. Marty Mann was the NCADD Washington, DC affiliate using the AA treatment as its vehicle working with over 3,000 hospitals. Let's remember that politics can mean the use of power of position to influence change."

Then and now these groups utilize people who have media strength to effect great change and directly influence the masses.

By 1980 AA through the NCADD had 223 affiliate relationships and 23 states had bought the disease idea mandating insurance coverage of alcoholism treatment. Their crusade had taken root and spread.

If the president of the United States isn't enough and U.S. government funding doesn't qualify as political, let's add AFL-CIO president George Meany and General Motors director James M. Roche as the NCADD all-star management committee.

In 1970 Congress passed the Hughes Act which gave incentive money to hospitals and organizations. Marty Mann and the AA organization had its major victory and had opened an office in Washington, DC.

Currently the number of organizations that AA and the NCADD are affiliated with are in the thousands. As a matter of fact the NCADD requests a percentage of the affiliates' earnings and one of AA's major profit centers is the revenue stream from its books and literature that these very organizations use. These relationships and affiliations are the life blood of AA's and NCADD's existence.

We know Marty Mann was the first woman in AA and founded the NCADD. The NCADD doesn't even try to hide the fact that it's directly involved with AA. This is right on the NCADD website. Let's not believe this is some coincidence. NCADD is just another front for AA.

NCADD flat out reveals its affiliate relationships while AA is extremely crafty about its word usage and professional relationships so as not to seem too obvious. Below are just a few of the facilities with NCADD/AA affiliation.

- Hazelden Foundation
- Betty Ford Center
- Hanley Center
- Robert Wood Johnson Founation
- Michael's House -The Treatment Center for Men
- Oxford House
- Phoenix House
  (From the NCADD website)

There are millions of dollars being exchanged and also direct profits going to AA from these relationships. This is no hidden thing almost all of these references are right there on the NCADD website which is a direct affiliation.

It's pretty clear to see that AA has a very strong involvement and is allied with politics, dozens of organizations and institutions, they always have been. This has been well documented year after year after year.

Let's take a look at **"not allied with any sect, denomination."** This will blow your mind!

The founders of AA, Bill and Bob got sober in the Oxford Group lead by cult leader Frank Buchman. This cult leader was also into what he called GOD-Control and Superhumanistism.

I don't know about you but that sounds pretty scary. Bill Wilson founder of AA originally didn't want to be tied to Buchman but there was one problem; the ideals and steps of AA are based on Buchman's work, the Fundamentalist First Century Christian Movement. So he really didn't have a choice.

Looking at Buchman's history he had such a sketchy background. Take a look at a few things from Frank's life and the Fundamentalist First Century Christian Movement, the Oxford Group Movement, or Moral Re-Armament (MRA).

As an ordained Lutheran minister Buchman had a great way of convincing people to follow his lead. He also had a reputation for prying into young men's lives, so much so that he was asked to move out of the men's dorm at the Hartford Seminary at the age of 38. The same troubles occurred for Buchman at Princeton.

Buchman's ways were known as Buchmanism, he was known as an evangelistic religious zealot. If you went against him your difference of opinion was met with anger, harsh words and considered to be evil and working for the Devil.

Additionally the faculty at Penn State said, "Buchman oozed the oil of unctuous piety from every pore and we would not be interested in seeing him again if it were at the cost of having to shake hands with him."

It's again clear to us AA is allied directly with cult work; in fact its foundation is built on the Fundamentalist First Century Christian Movement.

So with all the factual evidence combined with all the smoke around this guy's history would you trust him or his methods with your kids, your wife or husband?

Last but not least is **"does not wish to engage in any controversy, neither endorses nor opposes any causes."** It has been my personal experience that in a meeting of Alcoholics Anonymous if a subject is brought up that goes cross grain with the AA program it is met with great resistance and I've been often told by the old-timers during and after the meeting in AA rhetoric that my "type of program and beliefs" would only fail and to not discuss these ideas at the meetings.

Funny, these negative and direct threats are very similar to the tactics used by cult leader and AA influencer Frank Buchman.

I hope with all the above irrefutable evidence not much more is needed, however, if that wasn't enough let me take you to what nationally recognized historian, native Australian and oft-quoted 23-year Alcoholics Anonymous member and archivist Mitchell K. has to say in a summary of some of his articles sharing the troubles of a few actual persons overseas in the program and their unfortunate experiences.

These are Mitchell K's articles in condensed form which state several key things worth noting:

"First an AA veteran member has been ostracized by AA his sobriety and much more is now in jeopardy he has been sued by AA to the tune of $305,000 in addition may be looking at jail time and has been banned from going to any AA meeting or help other members. All this related to AA's world offices deviating from the pledge not to let money, property and the idea of not engaging in controversy override the central offices desire" for money. **Mitchell K. articles**

This AA member was a group leader in his hometown in Germany. He translated and printed the first 164 pages of the AA's Big Book as a means to help others who speak his native German tongue. This member personally picked up the tab for printing and was distributing the books for free in treatment centers, jails and prisons all the while thinking he was serving AA's primary purpose which was to carry the message to the alcoholic who still suffered.

At first look you might say this could be a straightforward copyright issue however after finding out more AA doesn't hold the copyrights any longer because the organization let them lapse, which places the book in the public domain.

Even with that being the case AA had taken this member to the fullest extreme that the law would allow. I suppose AA assumed that they could win. I don't know what they thought but it opened Pandora's Box. AA's bad practices have caught up with it and now all those who have been taken to court in the past over copyright cases can now file suit against AA dipping into their over $10 million prudent reserve they conveniently say they don't have.

Mitchell K. goes on to talk about AA tradition which states that AA will not accept outside contributions. But again this is not the case. AA accepted donations from the Rockefellers, however more than half of that money immediately went to pay Dr. Bob's (AA founder) house mortgage and the balance went to the founding members of AA. In addition to this AA accepted $250,000 from the city of San Diego, California, in 1995 and had plans to accept $100,000 from Minnesota so the AA conventions would come to their areas and spend money in their cities. Accepting these donations is a direct violation of AA's seventh tradition. What this says to AA members is heck if the founding members bend the rules they made themselves why can't we?

The last topic that I want to cover of Mitchell K.'s is something that I found to be of great importance. There is supposed to be an AA principle of attraction rather than the idea of promotion to gain members, but really they go much further than that. It starts with the idea of forcing someone to go to meetings. Mitchell writes himself that Americans have their introduction to AA by being forced to attend. He says in America we've become blinded to other models of treatment for alcoholism and addiction. He also says this "one eyed approach" will do AA great harm as all those past court cases against AA plainly show.

By court cases he means what happened in Australia. In Australia AA and NA (Narcotics Anonymous) controlled the alcoholism and addiction field and an investigation was done that revealed that almost every professional and counselor in the drug field was an NA member.

Mitchell states that "AA is the only way" got up the noses of the doctors, the governmental funding sources and the community agencies. From this investigation an official house cleaning was done and the dogmatic AA and NA were pushed out, governmental funding was reallocated and a more balanced approach won the day. The narrow focus of AA/NA lost their dominance and rigidity and the "we have the only way" was replaced with a more acceptable approach. Their perceived arrogance, jobs for AA/NA mates and seemingly holier-than-thou attitudes were tossed.

Mitchell K's prediction for the USA is: "As court cases continue to pile up because of forced attendance and religion issues there will be a backlash to pay." Mitchell's thoughts on how to head this off were to "bend over backward for atheists, non theists and humanists and more open ways by avoiding the trappings of 'you must go to meetings' and the religion push."

In closing on Mitchell K's articles, he states "I won't hold my breath the USA will be this sensible."

In Australia and other countries God is removed, there is no Lord's Prayer and you go to meetings because you want and choose to, therefore keeping the rooms more accessible for all religious and nonreligious people, thus keeping them in freedom.

WOW... after reading that ask yourself the question; does AA not wish to engage in any controversy, neither endorse nor oppose any causes? They may not wish to, however they sure don't have a problem railroading one of their own and greatly deviating from their "primary purpose" which is "to stay sober and help other alcoholics to achieve sobriety" instead of engaging in controversy and in this case opposing their own cause.

Let's look at the last statement in the AA preamble: **"Our primary purpose is to stay sober and help other alcoholics to achieve sobriety."** Based on my experience with the groups I've been involved with it is my belief this is absolutely true and the best intentions are kept in mind—for the most part. So how is it so many of the above stories happen in the mainstream treatment world?

It is so sad to me that most members have been convinced (brainwashed, if you will, from a cult-based program design) that AA is the only way! And that no new technologies in medicine will ever supersede the AA doctors' opinion or AA program. Additionally when other recovery approaches show results, marginally more successful than AA, it is said they are just a short-term fluke and these people are destined to relapse. Based on their track record, comparing it to many other treatment programs out there, how on earth can one possibly say it's the only way?! This is the 21st century. Why continue down an ancient road to find the answers we need for today?

CHAPTER FIVE

HOW PEOPLE GET HOOKED ON AA AND WHY THEY STAY WITH IT

....

After all those years sitting in the rooms I finally asked myself the question, why are these people in here every single day, year after year after year? From what I could see many who had stayed with the program were maintaining good periods of sobriety but most of their lives weren't getting better in any balanced kind of way. Clearly they were not fulfilling their life dreams—not even close. In fact to me it looked like the pilot light had gone out for most of these people and they seemed to have settled for a life of mediocrity.

What would make someone do this? Why would someone who knows they need to pay attention and learn more about handling their family life, health, career, etc, choose a lesser option? Don't they want more?

For example in many cases you would see people who badly needed to focus on bettering their health such as losing some weight because of high blood pressure. But instead they choose to ignore that issue, staying in poor health because they can't make the time or look beyond staying sober. Staying sober is the number one priority and they can't seem to grasp more than what AA puts on their plate which has all been accepted through the mediocre lives of those around them in the rooms thus making it seem ok. Maybe someone needed to focus on their relationship with their spouse, giving it more time and attention, but instead they go and share their issues with the people/person in the rooms, forgoing trying to include their spouse and reconnect at home. This generally will not fix the problem let alone make your spouse feel loved or included.

Another big issue I saw a lot of was flat-out broke people coming into the rooms month after month, year after year, never seeing their financial situation change a bit. But as long as they were clean, AAers would push that that was the only thing that mattered. I knew these people were fully capable of doing great things! But they were never motivated to do much more than stay sober. Which is okay, I guess; if that's the life you want. However clearly there is so much more available, so much more possible.

I saw good, intelligent and worthy person after person lower their standards after entering the rooms and stay on the same growth path, never getting their groove back toward life mastery or a healthy/wealthy fulfilling life. WHY?

One of my mentors Tony Robbins introduced me to the principle of the six human needs. After years of being in the rooms of AA I now see how the program hooks and keeps people in that environment of mediocrity.

Based on my research only a few of these six needs is required to be met for a sense of fulfillment to be attained in a given life situation. The six human needs are:

- Certainty / Comfort
- Significance
- Growth
- Uncertainty / Variety
- Connection / Love
- Contribution

Within the rooms of AA all of these needs exist. Let's address each one and see how it applies to the individual, to a group and its mediocrity that accepts you sober or not, working or not and growing in life or not.

Let me first say this: Acceptance of everyone is extremely important to me and I do accept everyone where they are but it is not the main focus or point of this chapter. I just really want to see people get the truth so they can grow in their own lives no matter where they are! It's mind boggling to witness how people get wrapped up in this and stay with it year after year, hardly bettering themselves beyond a sober life, *yet* they seem to be totally fine with it! We as humans are capable of so much more and we need to know that!!!

So let's take a look at these six human needs within the rooms of AA.

■ *Certainty/Comfort*—When you walk into a meeting you're almost always going to be greeted warmly and with open arms no matter what you look like or what's going on for you, exceptions made to some I suppose. However there is for sure a meeting out there that would love to have you.

You can be certain that there will be a person there with a story worse than yours, newcomers that will have very impactful stories and many, many drunk-a-logs. You can be certain in these rooms that there will be some kind of craziness, strong differences of opinion expressed, arguments and fights every now and again. It certainly is not lacking in the drama department. You can rest assured and take comfort in the fact that you'll also hear some great stories of life and about families that we can all relate to.

■ *Significance*—In just a few short weeks you will feel a part of the group knowing that you're playing a significant role in helping yourself and others by being a dependable fixture in the rooms. You feel significant for sure by being available for others 24/7 via phone, sharing your experiences, strengths, hopes, by having people come up to you or call you and ask for you to sponsor them, you feel needed. Flash forward a year or even just a few months and, man, forget about it, you are hooked! You feel like you're making a difference within that environment and for many they really do.

■ *Growth*—For some people just making it into the rooms is a huge step and if they are able to remain sober this is for certain major growth! The fact that you are required to read, comprehend and live by the 12 steps and the Big Book is also evidence of growth for many out there. I am not looking down on these achievements whatsoever. But I am wary of the lack of growth beyond all that. It is almost an illusion of growth for the member who is so caught up in the fantasy of getting better the AA way they cannot see the forest for the trees. Beyond getting and staying sober this is where there is a serious lack of balance in growing in one's life!

■ *Uncertainty/Variety*—Within the AA environment uncertainty and variety are the name of the game. There is always something going on at these meetings. Whether it be drama and chaos before, during or after the meeting just take your pick. It is there in abundance! The bottom line is there is no shortage of variety in these rooms, it is soap opera city!

■ *Connection/Love*—This is one area that I personally had a hard time giving up. I have met some of the best people that I know today in these rooms. Some of the connections that are made there can be very strong and on a deep level, especially when you all share something as profound as abusive drinking and addiction.

■ *Contribution*—I see this from two angles. When you come into the rooms you're contributing to the folks who have been there a while by helping them remember what it was like during the drinking days and in the newly sober days. The other side is after you're fully indoctrinated into the program you now contribute and give back by helping others and even "sponsor" those who are new to the program. I know for me after a short period of time I felt a loyalty to the rooms and the folks in them and since people pleasing and being accepted were a few of my major personal needs/hang-ups, I was vested completely. I personally understand how people get sucked right in! But for me at the same time I was conflicted! I knew something just wasn't quite right...what a spot to be in.

In conclusion to the six human needs as unveiled in AA:

I believe too many vulnerable and needy members fall right into the seductive arms of AA and have all their needs met way too quickly. Their needs are deceptively met in an unhealthy manner which does not breed equilibrium in the growth of one's life, thus making it super hard to see beyond the rooms. AA and the formal program do not provide a balanced curriculum for a well-rounded growing experience. How can it if all it focuses on is putting down the bottle and nothing beyond that?

With things such as:

- Indoctrination bordering on brainwashing
- Misinformation and deceit
- Deep immersion (90 meetings in 90 days)
- Ego destruction through self-criticism and confession sessions
- Thought-stopping clichés and slogans
- Guilt induction
- Wallowing in guilt
- Shame and self-contempt
- ("Stuff Your Feelings") Pretending to get positive results ("Fake It until You Make It")
- Confessions of powerlessness, insanity, sinfulness, selfishness, resentments and many other things, even driving people to suicide.

(Taken from the Orange papers http://www.orange-papers.org/orange-effectiveness.html)

However folks in the hundreds of thousands stay in these rooms, bound to the program like robots. Looking at the six human needs helps that makes sense to me. I will say this for the 5% that stay with the program and make positive use of it, many lives can get better in the rooms, but better to what standard? The problem is that the program doesn't expect it of them! It's in their best interest to keep us sick and coming back for more. So we get what we expect, nothing more and often less!

Is it realistic to believe that people's lives could get better in all ways, not just abstinence from drink/drug? Of course all areas are positively affected by abstinence. Anyone can see how eliminating overindulgence from one's life will positively affect you. Health, clearer-mindedness, no longer a threat to yourself, society or your family, stability for work, etc, but just think how much more it could be if we focused on a holistic and well-rounded picture for our healing! It could take you to the life that you dreamed of long ago but never imagined possible!

Another reason that this could be continuing is the big C word: Cult. If you had said this to me when I was new in the rooms I would have been really upset. But as time went on it got clearer and clearer what I was really seeing. I saw that I was part of a cult world that had sucked me in, along with so many others around me, and it was going on right before my eyes! A few didn't buy into it, a large number didn't know they bought into it and many were hard core all the way.

Let's look at the definition of "cult" in Webster's dictionary.
Main Entry: cult
Function: noun
Usage: often attributive
Etymology: French & Latin; French culte, from Latin cultus care, adoration, from colere to cultivate —
1: formal religious veneration: worship

2: a system of religious beliefs and ritual; also: its body of adherents

3: a religion regarded as unorthodox or spurious; also: its body of adherents

4: a system for the cure of disease based on dogma set forth by its promulgator <health cults>

5a: great devotion to a person, idea, object, movement, or work (as a film or book); especially: such devotion regarded as a literary or intellectual fad b: the object of such devotion c: a usually small group of people characterized by such devotion

Promulgator

1: to make (as a doctrine) known by open declaration: proclaim

2a: to make known or public the terms of (a proposed law) b: to put (a law) into action or force

synonyms see **declare**

I will tell you the exercise of writing this book has been so freeing! The truth will set you free for sure and for me not only has it done just that through the process of deprogramming my brain, but as the great E. James Rohn says, "The truth not only sets you free, but it positions you to be free to see your errors in judgment."

I consider the first half of this book to be the "deprogramming" phase. The deprogramming of the brain is absolutely crucial for a completely successful and sustained reawakening from a supposed coma in AA or other cult-like groups.

Based on the Webster's definition of cult, it fits to a tee! In Webster's word "cult," "cultivate" is used as the root word. It's a great way to describe what happens. People are cultivated along, conditioned to believe and do only as they (AA) do, to know no other way, to investigate no other resources, ultimately to completely give themselves over to the program and believe it is the best and only way.

When I came across the word "promulgator," I had to look it up—"to put into action or force." As mentioned in earlier chapters if you choose a different way in the rooms you are not welcome, you're either spoken to after a meeting or often shunned out. Now, if the program really had teeth people wouldn't have to radically force their ways on people, would they?

"Whether you think you can,
or think you can't, you're probably right."
– Henry Ford

Here's an example of what I've personally seen happen to people after they've been in AA for even a short period of time.

They receive the full indoctrination and are completely brainwashed. They believe that they are powerless, sick or different than other people and that the program is the solution to most everything. Yes you've heard of Gamblers Anonymous, Clutters Anonymous, Nicotine Anonymous, Overeaters Anonymous, Debtors Anonymous, Sex Addicts Anonymous and the list goes on. Okay so when the person is working on their issues they gain a little traction and then something goes wrong in their lives, boom! They say, I knew it! I'm powerless, I'm sick, I'll never be able to handle or fix the problem! I need the program for this issue! They either go back to the same group to share their tale of woe or join another Anonymous group where again they're told, yup you have a disease it can't be fixed. The best you can hope for is to be arrested or go into remission through working the steps. This is what is referred to as **learned helplessness.** Powerlessness is indoctrinated and now the person is totally screwed!

Did you know a control test was done by Dr. Jeffrey Brandsma who found that people who used AA as a form of recovery where *five* times more likely to binge drink or a have a full-blown relapse than those who got sober on their own *and nine* times more likely than those who learned to change their behaviors?

Maybe it's because of all the guilt that is put upon you in the rooms or the insane idea that relapse is part of recovery. Maybe it's the loss of control and "strange mental blank spots" that are cultivated into the mind of the mainstream treatment patient. Can you see how this falls directly into the category of "As a man thinketh, so is he"?

To get more clarification on cults let's ask a professional the direct questions: What are cults and what do they do? Then you can decide for yourself if AA sounds like a cult community.

"Cults serve diverse purposes for individuals. These purposes include providing a positive sense of community where values are focused, affirmed, and reinforced. The relationship among individuals in a cult is also hypnotic (Freud 1959; Becker 1973). Individuals who disagree with an ideology binding individuals together in a group are likely to be criticized, punished, and eventually excluded or shunned by the group. The first rule of the cult is 'thou shalt not disagree.' Affiliation and membership in the cult rests on establishment and maintenance of an ideology consensus. For the cult to maintain its singular identity, the rule must be obeyed. Break the rule and you break the spell. In order for a singular group identity to persist, individual identities must be contained."

– Addiction Is a Choice by Dr Schaler

"It has been widely recognized by social scientists that AA itself is a classic cult. Sociologists Greil and Rudy looked at the process of conversion to the AA world-view, and concluded that involvement with AA is more likely to involve a high degree of coercion than other cases of religious conversion (1983, p 23) the central dynamic in the AA conversion process is being brought to accept the opinions of AA, not just about drinking but about life in general. The process of individual recruitments to AA 'entails a radical transformation of personal identity,'

*in that the AA message 'provides the prospective affiliate not
merely with a solution to problems related to drinking, but also
with an overarching world view with which the convert can and
must reinterpret his or her past experience."*

- Addiction Is a Choice by Dr Schaler

"The simplest way to test whether a group of people who think
alike is a cult is to see how they respond to disagreement to
their core beliefs. Most cults tolerate disagreement over pe-
ripheral issues, but come down furiously on any dissent from
the core principles. Cults usually follow practices, such as the
'thought terminating cliché' (Lifton 1961) to close off certain
dangerous lines of discussion. Often, members will be scorned,
or worse, for reading dangerous books or having contacts
with dangerous individuals. The stronger the evidence against
the cult's core beliefs, the more emotional and inflexible the
response to presentation of that evidence. The worst cults discourage social interaction between members and outsiders."

- Addiction Is a Choice by Dr Schaler

In order to finally close the coffin on *why we've been lied to,* let me
give you 200 billion reasons...let's look at who's making the money.

Again, when I started this project more and more things started to
come to the surface seemingly by themselves. I knew that the treatment
facilities and insurance companies would love to see people sick and keep
them in there supposed care. I knew that they would manipulate patients
and patients' families so all things would point to the patient coming
back to their facility, but why?

Okay, so remember they'll have you believing alcoholism is an allergy
of the mind, an obsession of the body and an outright disease, right? And
that relapse is a part of recovery. This is why they say you'll be back and

it's best at their facility because they know the patient's needs best as they were already in their care. That would be nice if it were all true but let's look at the real driving force.

Money! Money! Money! And lots of it! As I said earlier when I started this project more and more things started to come to the surface and this topic of money was no exception. One day I was doing some keyword and pay-per-click word selecting for my company's website. (This is where you select the best words that are most searched for via search engines such as yahoo, google, ask.com, msn, etc. The pay-per-click advertising piece is where you pay for each time someone clicks on a search word you've paid for, driving them directly to your site.)

There are several different tools you can use to make sure you don't overpay for your words and your positioning. This is simple and straight-forward I hope.

My company provides tools and training for the military and law enforcement communities, so keywords and phrases like combat, special forces, knife training, edged weapons defense are keywords I would bid for and purchase.

So I started my working session. Words within my industry range from 40 cents to the max at about $1.50 and the competition for these words was at about 50-65%. I felt a little curious so I started looking at other industries such as fitness, health, dieting, wealth building etc. Their keywords went for anywhere from $3.50 on up to $8, competition for these words was at about 65-80%.

Then it hit me. Why don't I see how much treatment centers are paying for words such as alcoholism, addiction, rehab, treatment centers, etc. These words started at $15 per click and were $25 at the high end, and competition for these words was at 100% per word per click! It blew my mind.

As a businessman this was very telling. If an organization can afford to pay $15 per word per click on one area of their business-marketing plan their profit margins have to be through the roof. Nothing says more about the strength of an industry than what an organization is willing to pay for advertising and marketing. This is an area that will drain and kill a business faster than any other area of expense because it is crucial that they get an RIO (return on their investment).

After doing even more research I wanted to find out exactly how big the pie was, so to speak. At the writing of this book the alcohol and drug treatment industry is a $200 billion enterprise WOW! No wonder people do what they do to control it. There is an astronomical amount of money in it!!!

Well the whistle has been blown on the treatment facilities. They are making a killing. So why don't they help people achieve the best of their abilities? It's quite simple. It's not in the industry's best interest! These facilities get TONS more money by keeping people sick rather than getting them well, period!

So, if you're half as human I am, I hope you're good and mad.

I'll tell you I was so pissed off when I found out about all of this. I knew the best thing I could do was to keep moving my life in the direction that I wanted to take it and not look back. The only problem was I was still mad as hell and had to do something with that anger.

In the next chapter we will go through the processes of getting beyond the pains of the past and moving forward in life.

CHAPTER SIX

LETTING GO OF THE PAIN OF BEING LIED TO, MOVING FORWARD AND BEYOND TO A SIGNIFICANTLY BETTER LIFE

· ·

Can you imagine how I felt after suspecting something wasn't quite right deep down inside with the AA rooms but not knowing what it was? I felt this after being involved for only a short time. But almost a full decade went by before I truly started putting it all together for myself.

This is where I would like to introduce the second key:

Power Baseline (PBL)

Your power baseline's foundation is the TPK (true perspective knowledge) but on top of that is knowing what people are successfully doing to create an addiction-free life. This is your power baseline. Once you know all the methods that are available, the results people are getting, read the stories and visit the websites, organizations and resources, you will be able to move forward with *power*. This is the position of advantage! My mentors tell me that many quality aspects of life are like the combination to a secret vault. The contents inside are very valuable and people will perform all sorts of craft to prevent anyone from getting to it. However through careful observation, asking questions, quiet reflection, tons of reading, being open to new ideas, researching the relevant data, looking at results from other people and most of all looking for a better life for my family, I found the correct numbers to life's secret vault! I put them in the correct sequence and voila, the vault opened. That was the day the big paradigm shift occurred for me. On that day I went from being a victim to a victor!

However, a by-product of this was the very real fact that I was pissed! All of these years of investing major time, energy and emotion—wasted! The thoughts that went through my head ran the gamut but in the end I was mostly mad at myself for not trusting my gut and what I felt I knew all along. Mad for not checking first and doing the homework myself, for not being a student but a follower. Then the "I should haves" started settling in. I should have done this and I should have done that and you know what they say about "should-ing" all over yourself, you only end up with more pain. I found out that hurt people hurt people.

One thing is for sure, folks like us with abuse issues know how to dig up the past! We blame somebody or something, hit ourselves over the head with a baseball bat, talk about the good old days, the bad old days, about tomorrow, anything but live in the now. Heck we've even been known to brag about it. I remember once in the rooms a gal told this story with great gusto about how she drove home after being at a bar and crashed into five of her neighbors' parked cars! She seemed almost proud to have the story to share with all the AAers. Then of course the next guy tells his gruesome drunk story of swinging his son in circles and letting go by mistake, then his son goes smashing into the wall, bashing his face and breaking his arm. Then the next crazy drinking story follows and so on... unbelievable! Please tell me how is this going to help us stop abusing ourselves if we're constantly reliving these stories with intensity and emotion, strengthening the brain's associations with these events?

All it's going to do is make us anxious and bring up thoughts and feelings closely associated with the events. Responsively we start to live closer to those old behaviors. Behaviors we want to forget. Times when we were obnoxious and disgusting, times when we embarrassed our families, when we were rude, slutty, stupid, told lies, degraded ourselves and the ones we love, etc... This brings on more feelings of guilt, fear, remorse and depression which works like having a big anchor behind you, pulling you back, weighing you down as you struggle to get ahead. Hardly seems like the road to a healthy recovery. And it isn't.

A big part of creating a new life is moving away from the old one for good. Yes we should remember what the results are from our past actions to the degree that we are aware of the consequences but emotionalizing it and reliving it over and over and over again does in my opinion more harm than good. Know where you've been, acknowledge it—then move on!!!

I now see my old drinking and drug behaviors as a distant bad memory, a time when I did stupid things and made mistakes—period. The way it plays out for me now is knowing that if I choose drinking or drugging it's like choosing to drive my car the wrong way down a one-way street or willfully driving off the side of the road down a rocky cliff. I just don't do it! I don't have to have a major mental gymnastics exercise over it.

Yes in the beginning I had to think about it more but it quickly became a natural thought process like riding a bike—you learn what to do and you just do it. You don't have to talk about it over and over or make a call to somebody to tell you not to turn down that one-way street. No, you—**you**—make that decision! It's your life and you are responsible for it! It really is that simple. But if you have a diseased belief system nothing is simple.

We are going to use a similar technique for getting beyond the hurts, hang-ups, past pains, life issues and bad behaviors as we move beyond the pain of being lied to. These can be used for any issue, challenge, person, etc, in your life. I wanted to include this tool because it is very simple yet very powerful. (In part 2 this is the exercise I'll be referencing.)

Initially I might think and say that I wish that _____event never happened. And that would be nice, however that's not reality and I or you can't go back in time. There's not a single thing we can change about our past except the way we think about it. It's over and done with and we must put it in the past where it belongs!

In order to achieve this there are several different methods we can use to move beyond the past negative events in our lives that are still haunting us. I'm going to suggest a few methods that are very powerful and have worked for both me and others very well.

The first method is a technique I learned from Jack Canfield, author of *Chicken Soup for the Soul*. Jack has an outstanding success-building program that includes something called the Total Truth Process and the Total Truth Letter. Both these processes work to help release the anger and emotions that are not serving us and help us get back on track within our lives and to a state of power.

It's been my experience that when we're mad we won't share the full story or all the emotion of our feelings with the person/group that we're mad at. This keeps us in a stall and we don't move past it through the ranges of emotions. The result often being a varying "dis"-ease with the person/group.

The overall goal of any release process is to let go of what is binding us up. We should want to be in a state of general joy, peace and acceptance. This is one place where true power comes from—this is a place we want to be.

The elements of verbalizing or writing a letter are the same. The idea is to go through the range of feelings and get to a place of forgiveness and peace. You will either write all these feelings in a personal letter (the Total Truth Letter) to later dispose of or you will find a partner to verbalize your feelings to. You can also have your partner do the exercise along with you; this is very beneficial for those you carry resentment in relationships or anger towards one another about the past or certain events. Remember it is crucial that you move through the anger, fear, resent-ments and finish in a place of forgiveness and peace. If it takes you more than once to get there that is just fine. Some of us are holding onto a lot!!!

If you do this exercise verbally make sure you and the other party both are clear with the guidelines of the drill and aren't going to just lay into each other with all the venom of a king cobra. I can promise you it will not be a successful exercise that way.

For this exercise to be effective spend equal time in each stage. You can use the sentence starter ideas below.

1. Anger, frustration and resentments
    I'm angry with...
    I'm frustrated that...
    I hate it when you...
    I'm upset with this organization because...

2. Offended, hurt and upset
    It hurt me when...
    I was offended that...
    I feel disappointed that...

3. Regret, disappointment, remorse, distress
    I'm sorry that...
    Forgive me for...
    I didn't like the way...

4. Wants, desires and wishes
    I feel that...
    What I would like to see is ...
    All I ever wanted was...

5. Compassion, forgiveness and appreciation

I understand that...
I forgive you for...
I appreciate....

I was so angry with past issues I needed to find a safe way to purge my feelings. I found myself writing several letters with all five elements of the Total Truth Process.

The biggest no-no in this drill is to not do it! You will for sure yield ZERO results! I know it may seem very simplistic but *do not underestimate the power of this exercise!* This is a key part on the path to your own personal freedom. This step in the process is HUGE!!!

As with all things in life we must put the effort forth. I'm always taken aback when I see people who have many wants in life but who are not willing to put in the hard work necessary to achieve those wants. I can tell you straight away the path in this book is a way that you will build massive results for yourself and your loved one but you **must do the work!** This is not a "sit and be a wallflower and expect results" path. You'll have to put OUT the effort—however it's far less effort once you've gotten yourself moving and gained momentum. Trust me if you do this the end results will be mind bending!

Okay, now that we've done the Total Truth exercise either verbally or in writing you'll want to take a few minutes to relax and acknowledge the good work you've done. You can even give yourself a small reward for your effort—go get that Starbucks coffee, buy a new book, have a great relaxing meal with your partner by candlelight, whatever would make you feel rewarded—an "ah, yes I've accomplished this" feeling! We're taking control of our lives by letting go of these bad past experiences and moving on. If the thoughts come up again (and they will) know that you've done the work to move on from them and do just that, move forward! You may have to do the letter again and again. But my suggestion is to just move forward. You've done the letting go/release work so again do just that, trust yourself and let go!

NOTES

NOTES

PART TWO

. . . .

GETTING BACK ON TRACK AND BEYOND

CHAPTER SEVEN

WHAT IS RECOVERY?

· ·

I n order to get anywhere we must know where we are going. We must have an idea of our end game. So I ask you, what is recovery to you? This question brought on some more homework for me, so the first place I went was Webster's dictionary. The Webster's definition is:

Re·cov·er·y

1. An act of recovering.
2. The regaining of or possibility of regaining something lost or taken away.
3. Restoration or return to health from sickness.
4. Restoration or return to any former and better state or condition.
5. Time required for recovering.
6. Something that is gained in recovering.
7. An improvement in the economy marking the end of a recession or decline.
8. The regaining of substances in usable form, as from refuse material or waste products.
9. The rising price of an asset. For example, following an extended decline in the price of precious metals, investor expectations of future inflation may generate recoveries in gold and silver prices.

One thing I found in common in most of these definitions was the notion of something going back to its original form so it can then grow and become better than before.

I spent some time searching on the Internet and in my library of recovery books, and what follows is the best definition that I found that resonated with my personal understanding of what recovery from alcohol and drug use means:

"Alcohol and drug addiction recovery is nothing short of living the life of your dreams."

That's a pretty straightforward statement. To me that's what recovery should be all about—living the life of your dreams. Getting not just back to where you were before but beyond.

This is what the second half of this book is about. Getting our destructive issues / habits / disempowering occurrences / so-called diseases behind us. Call it whatever you want, I don't care. We're talking about putting it in the rearview mirror and watching it disappear forever.

If we look closely at anything in life that we want or want to achieve, the best way to go about it is to set a goal and then move backward to engineer the solution to it. This is plan development.

Example 1. You want to send your kids to college. Option A: You get a solid idea of what the costs are and then go to work years earlier to properly save for it. Option B: Hope your kids earn scholarships and say to yourself, we'll figure it out when we get there.

Example 2. You want that expensive beach house. Option A: You need to save X amount of dollars each month for so many years until you have enough for a down payment. Option B: Perhaps your family and three other families can put together X amount of dollars and then you'll only have to lease out the house to seasonal renters for a few months out of the year. Option C: Just think about your dreams and hope it will all come together someday.

I hope you get my point here. If we want to achieve anything worth-while winging it and dreaming about it will not cut it. I'm not saying you can't be loose but you must have a guide to follow, a proven path to the results that you're after. Winging it, sitting around dreaming about it and talking about the good old days definitely will not do it.

We know that even in some of the best environments great people still don't succeed in the attainment of their dreams. Why not? A big part of it is the winging-it plan for success. Another name is the "just get by" plan or the "I'll know it when I see it" plan, which takes us down Someday Road to a city called Nowhere Ville in How'd we get here Township. Got it?

I cannot focus on this enough. We *must* have some type of key plan that works with the other parts of your life to form a complete holistic, balanced existence. Only then can we go further and faster with less effort.

If we want to have that life that we dreamed of then we must STOP. Stop, take a deep breath and say, I'm going to change my life TODAY. Not tomorrow, RIGHT NOW! Make that *decision*, then turn toward your new life and start RUNNING in that direction. The word decision comes from the Latin *decisio*, meaning, *literally, a cutting off!* Make that decision now, cut yourself off from the old you and start anew!!!

Swear this oath to yourself: I accept no excuses in my attitude and I swear to do my very best with all my actions! If I fall down (and I will fall down) I will pull myself up by my bootstraps and dust myself off. I swear to keep going in the direction of my new life. Why? Because it's my new life! Yes, stuff's going to happen, but SO WHAT? That was THEN, this is NOW! Just because it happened in the past does not mean it will happen in the future! My time is now!

> *"It is our thinking that makes it so!"*
>
> - Greek philosopher

You may be saying, what that's it?! That's all I have to do? And I say to you—Yes! To get the master blueprint it starts with going in the right direction. To make any change it begins with a decision and once that decision is made there is no looking back. This is why they don't make rearview mirrors the size of the front windows. You need to stay focused on where you're headed. In some race cars they don't even have rearview mirrors only side view for changing lanes so you don't collide with something coming up from behind you wanting to pass. If so you just wait till it passes or simply speed up. Pretty straightforward plan, not so easy if you're just wingin' it.

Listen, as I mentioned earlier in the book, I'm a pilot and there is only ONE time that you really use full power—during takeoff!

CHAPTER EIGHT

THE MASTER KEY TO THE LIFE YOU DESERVE: TAKING 100% RESPONSIBILITY FOR THE LIFE YOU WANT

· ·

The first thing to know is that the following is based on research and principles. Results don't lie. The principles work but you must put them to work, no one can do it for you. Can you imagine needing to get fit and asking someone else to do your pushups? Can you imagine wanting that promotion at work and hoping it will happen without impressing the boss or working overtime to get it? Can you imagine wanting to speak a new language without studying and going through the memory and gender exercises? It would never happen. You would have earned only one thing, frustration!

What is absolutely 100% necessary even amidst all the doubt that you feel, the taking charge and responsibility of your own life boils down to that one word, _decision._ In making the decision that you want this, believing that you deserve this and putting to work the proven methods and principles expecting nothing less than success for yourself is what it takes. If you learn this, immerse yourself in this and apply it with discipline every day, it will transform you and your life to baseline and beyond!

As you move forward through this material know that everyone learns differently and there are many ways you can apply the principles for your success.

My suggestion is to read all the material first so you can gain a sense for the whole process before you start designing the life that you truly want. Please remember these are in order and one principle builds on another. It's like getting dressed, underwear and socks go first, you wouldn't put your underwear over your pants or dress and you wouldn't put your socks over your shoes.

As you are reading, underline and highlight the things that jump out or are important to you. Depending on how you plan to use this you're going to want to re-read and remind yourself of what you must do to get to your goal. As you read you may say "I know that" but then ask yourself are you applying it to your life today? Additionally if you find yourself resisting or refusing to accept a principle, then this is probably one you need the most. Do your best to remain open minded and solution oriented.

If you've been exposed to traditional recovery you will probably need someone to support your new beliefs/actions and having an accountability partner is also a great idea. There are numerous resources available for these and they are mentioned toward the end of this book.

This is why the first part of the book is there—to deprogram the brainwashing and lies you've been fed. You'll be much better off letting go of that information from the mainstream. Remember first in, first on (This is a way to state that what is first taken into your brain will, generally take precedence). It's like being told something about someone you don't know there is a tendency to sway the way we think about that person true or not.

Reality check

Depending on your level and years of drinking or drug use and where you are in your mindset this is going to weigh heavy on your ability to make the transition faster or slower.

At first you may be very excited and enthused or you may be very skeptical and tentative. I urge you to trust that you do have a glimmer of hope. Trust it, believe in yourself and move forward without looking back. Everything that has led you to this moment is right on time. We as people do the best we can with the information that we have at that moment. And now you are learning more as each page turns and will be armed with loads and loads of proven information. Relax and enjoy the moment!

Your success will take time and it will be hard. Just like learning a new trade, a new sport, meeting a new person, nothing worthwhile is easy. If you are not committed like so many out there who give up, failure will be easy. Many times you may find that you have to recommit to your commitment.

Folks with true wisdom have discovered if you keep knocking someone will open the door. And at this moment if you do not give up you'll feel as if you made a quantum leap in your abilities and then in that moment you will know that—you have made that leap.

Patience is a virtue to be had, stay the course and DO NOT GIVE UP. Success will come to you in the uncommon hour. Principles don't lie!

Make today the day you turn your life around.

Grabbing the BULL by the horns

The keyword here is BULL. Yup, short for Bullshit. What I'm talking about here is this thought that the world owes us something. That this great life we're supposed to have is meant to be handed right to us on a platter. That somebody or something else is responsible for providing us with happiness, sobriety, a great career, a loving family, a balanced personal relationship and great health and fitness—simply because.

The rock-bottom truth is you and you alone are responsible for the quality of your life. We are not children any longer, no one else is responsible for us now, period.

If you want that life YOU must go out and get it. YOU must take 100% responsibility for achieving your goal. This applies greatly in the area of being clean and sober. No one else got us here except for us and we must get ourselves out of it. This doesn't mean we can't ask for and accept help, it's just not hinged on it. YOU CANNOT put the responsibility onto someone else.

The truth is most of us have been conditioned to put blame outside of ourselves for the areas in our lives that we don't like and to take credit only for the things we do like. Doesn't sound so straight does it?

Most of us don't want to look at where the real problem is "taking the BULL by the horns" and putting him down for good, that would be too hard. So most of us take the easy route—"It is our thinking that makes it so!" blame somebody, something, some event, anything but the real problem, ourselves!!!

Today is the day to say enough is enough, I'm going to get real right now, right this minute, I'm gonna make that decision, head in that new direction and never turn back.

What's more important in your life than the choice to get real?

This part really pissed me off when I started to look at it. I thought, "Am I saying the crazy, nasty and unforgivable things that happened to me when I was 2 years to 18 years old are all my fault?" Absolutely not! You are not to blame for any craziness you suffered as a child. What I am saying is that if you want the life you deserve, from now on you must take 100% responsibility for what's happened in your life since you became an adult. WOW! That's some big-time tall order, I know.

In the military, law enforcement and civilian courses that we teach at work, we have a phase of the training called joining the BBC—the Big Boys Club. This is where the students are expected to step up in a big way. And you know what? Almost everyone always does. The ones who slide back are in general those that don't have that "need to stay alive" commitment, which plays a big part in whether or not you join and *stay* in that club.

How do you know if you're slipping out of the club? You notice yourself making excuses and blaming things outside of yourself for circumstances in your life. You notice yourself complaining and forgetting to have an attitude of gratitude. Taking 100% responsibility for your life means you recognize that every decision you make as an adult has a consequence good or bad. We get to choose whether we *react* or *respond* to all of life's events and therefore set a stage and a tone for our life. It is up to us to make it what we want.

And if what you want is to be a major powerhouse you must stop blaming and complaining and take 100% responsibility for both your successes and failures. This is a HUGE step I know. It was for me.

For this to work you're going to have to take a stand and know that you always have the ability and power to make your life the way you want it to be. Whatever your reasons were for not taking action—lack of knowledge, low self-confidence, fear, the need to be right, the list goes on—don't matter now, the past is the past. What does matter is that you look forward to and take action toward your dreams. Of course a major part of that is leaving your substance use in the past where it belongs. Are you ready to join the BBC of self-truth, or will you stay in the safety zone of did and got what you got, that's why you are where you are? This can be a painful realization, however the truth often is. Are you going to hang with the turkeys or soar with Eagles?

This is all choice nothing more nothing less. Yes you'll definitely need support but once you make the choice to take 100% responsibility for yourself, all of this is going to be so much easier your head will spin! "Acting as if" can be a very powerful tool for you to use in any situation when you don't know what to do. All you do is "act as if" and then do the right thing, take 100% responsibility for the life that you want and go in that direction.

When something doesn't turn out the way you wanted, ask yourself a few questions. How did I allow this to happen? What did I believe at the time? What did I say or not say? What do I need to do different next time to get what I want?

You will never become successful as long as you continue to blame things outside yourself for your lack of success. If you plan to be a champion you have to identify the truth.

The day you change how you react to things will be a banner moment in your life.

When I was told that my thoughts feed my feelings which feed my words and actions, I heard it but I didn't take it to heart, which brings us to complaining. In order to have a complaint you must believe that something better is out there for you and your family. This means you have a point of reference that there's something else you prefer but are not willing to take responsibility for making it happen in your life.

Each time I focus, complain or bitch about something I remind myself of and re-create that event in my mind and body, bringing it closer to my life. I think it, I feel it, I say it or act it, I make it so. This can be a vicious circle to get out of unless you recognize that you're in it and have the correct backup plan.

Run this through your thought process... We really only complain about things we **can** do something about. We wish we lived in a better neighborhood, we complain about a car we have, we complain about our weight, we complain about not being able to take a vacation, we complain about the weather, where we live and so on.

These are all things we can change. You never hear anybody complaining about the planets, the color of the sky or gravity, do you? These things just are and we accept them as they are.

The things that we complain about we can change, however this would require that **we** change.

So why don't we take the necessary action? Is it the fear of failing, of being wrong or of confrontation? Either accept that you're okay with where you are in life or take the risk to make your life the way you want it. The worst that can happen is you'll have learned what doesn't work.

Today make the choice to stop bitching, to stop hanging out with complainers, and move forward with your life.

If you're to make the transition you must learn to replace complaining with asking. Asking for what you want and taking action to get what you want. This is the way of the successful man or woman. If you're in a place you don't want to be and you're not happy, make a decision to make it better or leave.

So many people just sit in their own crap and bitch and moan, boy don't let that be you. It's totally up to you to make the change. Nobody owes you anything, not the world, not a corporation, not the community. Our life is of our own making.

Know that we either allowed it to happen or we directly made it happen. Meaning that whatever it is in your life, it didn't just fall on you. You played a major role...a starring role! This may seem too harsh of a statement in relation to some of the situations that have happened to many of us. However if we want to find the power we must take the position that we are 100% responsible for ourselves now!

Let's be straight. We all know that probably a majority of the time we had an insight a feeling about somebody or something that was a dead giveaway but we failed to act on it. These wake-up calls are there for us to make a change in our direction of action (a course correction). However loads of people do not take action or listen to these insights and feelings, they act as if they don't see it coming and look the other way. In the short term it's so much easier to not deal with it because you don't have the confrontation, the discomfort, the work, etc, but in the end—well we all know how the story ends.

There is a much better course of action and that is to face life challenges head-on, sometimes taking action that is uncomfortable but gets us closer to our goal. Achievers don't wait for things to fall apart and then take action, they take action up front. Once you start acting this way it feels great! You feel the power that comes with being in control of the results in your life.

This is a straightforward request, what we have today is a result of what we did yesterday. To get the new life that we want we must do more action that moves us in that direction, this means feeding our minds with better information, saying, doing and taking better actions.

Just because it's straightforward doesn't mean it's going to be easy. In fact this will probably be one of the hardest but one of the best things that you'll ever do in your entire life.

Your awareness level is going to have to be higher, you're going to have to shoot for personal excellence, you're going to need to ask for feedback and look closely at the results that you're getting from your actions.

I'm going to suggest that once you make the commitment to change your life that you also make the commitment to slow yourself down a bit so you can make better decisions and smell the roses from those decisions. Also so you can raise your awareness level. This is exactly what we do to super-tune Warriors and Special Forces prior to being deployed onto the battlefield.

You're going to need to give up your disease of excusitis and square up with the results you're getting in your life today. Do a full 360-degree rotational view and ask, Is drinking, drugging, lying, gambling, cheating, your way through life really okay with you? Is your family life, your work, your level of health, your financial earnings, how you are living and your current abilities okay with you? If not what are you going to do about it?

Be square and honest with yourself—nothing less will do. This is what taking 100% responsibility really means!

CHAPTER NINE

CREATING UNSTOPPABLE DRIVE TO THRIVE: HAVING A NO-EXCUSES VISION AND PLAN FOR SUCCESS!

. . . .

If you can dream it you can achieve it! It was put on your heart for you, no one else but you. If you feel that burning desire it's meant for your attainment and nobody else's. The word desire means "a wish or longing," "to await what the stars will bring," "from the stars," "of the father, of spirit, from the heavenly body." I don't know about you but that's just as clear as day to me. It is yours! So now we must clear out all that junk in our brains, our body and our thought processes for good.

> *"It doesn't take any more effort to dream a big dream than it takes to dream a small dream."*
> — General Wesley Clark, Former Head of NATO

Again it's going to be next to impossible to make yard steps toward progress with a mindset that is fixed in the past. Past actions, past belief systems, past events, destructive ideas that say your mind is broken. Let me be really clear here, these aforementioned mental fixations will have you sabotaging your forward movement faster than flies on cow poop in the summer if you know what I mean.

These fixations will have you looking in the rearview mirror crashing into everything in front of you. Moving really slowly because your mind and vision are fixed on the "what I did" the "what he/she did" the "what he/she said" the "what happed to me" the "what I missed out on" the "how could they have done that to me?" the "you see I told you my mind and body was messed up, that's why this is happening to me" or "why this didn't happen for me" get my drift?

Did you ever look at a beautiful baby and say WOW so gorgeous, so connected to the heavens, so pure, so right? Then you look at the guy or girl next door or in the mirror and say what the hell happened?! What happened to that connectedness, that purity?

It did not leave *us, we left it!* The good news is that it is still there waiting for you with open arms saying, I was waiting for you to come back. I kept throwing you a line but you didn't want to have anything to do with me. So I've been waiting.

It can be retrieved in minutes if you would just connect with the desires of your heart. What have you been longing for? What do you know has always been meant for you? What have you really wanted to do? Who are you really inside? Remember, *"Recovery is nothing short of living the life of your dreams."*

It all starts with asking the question who am I really? Which is driven by what do I really desire? If it's been in your heart it's a part of you. Do not let anyone—**ANYONE**—tell you otherwise.

Please be prepared because the naysayers will come on strong. They have copped out of life and will feel threatened by you. They've settled in for a mediocre—less than—life. NEVER forget birds of a feather flock together and they will not want you leaving the pack. Because they copped out they will not want to see your success greater than their own. But life success is not classified just for a select few, it's for anybody! Anybody who says, "That's for me and I'm going to go get it no matter what!" No excuses, PERIOD!

Okay, how do we go about living the life of our dreams? The future really is created **now**. See it so you can achieve it. No buildings are built, no communities are made, fantastic lives are not had without a blueprint first! So let's start drawing the picture of our lives right now!

Will it be worth it? Yes.
Will it be outstanding? Yes.
Will you say I can't believe I did it? Yes.
Will it be hard? Yes.
Will it be easier if you have a road map? Yes.
Will you regret it if you don't try? Yes.
So what are you waiting for?

Fill in the blanks now to complete this exercise! Remember there are no wrong answers! Dream big and don't hold back for anything!!! Take as much time as you need do not wait...

What do you want from your relationship?
What do you want from your career?
What do you REALLY see yourself doing?
What type of home do you REALLY want?
What do you want from your fitness life/your health?
What do you want for your kids and grandkids?
What do you want people to say about you when you're gone?
What do you want to be remembered for?
What organizations do you want to contribute to? -
Where in the world do you want to go?
What languages do you want to speak?
Where do you want to make your biggest impact?
How much money do you want to make 1, 3, 5, 10, 20, 30 years from now? (Be specific.)

How many people do you want to help?

What part of the world REALLY speaks to you?

What can't you stand? What do you want to change?

What type of car do you REALLY want to drive?

What toys do you want?

Where do you want to live?

Who do you REALLY love?

Where do you REALLY want your kids to go to school?

What activities would you like to put your kids in?

Where do you REALLY want to go to school?

What do you REALLY want to eat?

What clothes do you REALLY want to wear?

Where do you REALLY want to have a vacation home?

What bills do you really want to pay off?

What do you REALLY want your backyard to look like?

What do you want your parents to say about you?

What do you want your friends to say about you? (Your real friends.)

How do you REALLY want to feel?

Who do you REALLY see yourself as?

What do you REALLY want to do with your time?

What do you want to give or treat your spouse to?

What do you want to do for that kid around the corner whose parents just don't get it?

Get the idea? Dream! And dream big! Forget the statement "Don't get your hopes up." Whoever heard of low hopes anyway?

This process must be written down for you to get the intended results, doing it in your head doesn't have nearly the same effect. Don't start the next phase of your life doing things halfway, start a new discipline!

As you're doing this expect things to start showing up, don't be surprised that better options for your life start presenting themselves. Don't be surprised when you start seeing that car that you want show itself more often when you're driving around. Don't be surprised if that dream job of yours is talked about by someone who can help you actually get that interview. By naming / writing down your goal you create a live energy connection that has your name on it!

Next is the power phase. In order for this thing to take off it must have power. That power lies in **why you want it**! Why do you want to send your kids to that school? Why do you want to live in that city? Why do you want to buy that safe car for your wife? Why do you REALLY feel that longing to go to the country where your parents grew up? Why do you REALLY feel the connection to that foundation that always runs their commercials just when you turn the TV on or before you go to bed? Why do you REALLY want to wear those clothes from that designer or that certain brand?

Because it makes you feel a certain way, a good way! Because it makes you feel alive! That's the way we're supposed to feel, **alive**! The more we feel alive the less we need fillers in our lives, the less we need to escape the less we need to change the way we are currently feeling, the more we grow up! Write each "why" down and keep them with your wants list. You will be referencing these daily. I would suggest buying yourself a nice journal to keep all of these precious thoughts in, safe and accessible.

This will be your start on being able to handle the lows of life and yes you will have them—but so what, we all do...**grow up**!

For right now use this picture that you've created and written down to empower you to go for something OUTSTANDING. Your mind is going to tell you all kinds of crap about why you can't do this, that you'll mess that up, that your brain is not capable of achieving it and even if you did you'd lose it anyway.

You know what? That's all bullshit!! Flat out bullshit! The past does not equal the future! If one man or woman can do it so can another and so can you!

Resolve to yourself that you will do it no matter what, even if your wheels fall off, even if it rains on your parade (and it will). Resolve that you will not stop striving for your destined life until you get there—**until** is the keyword. Picture your baby and how long would you give them until he or she walked? Would you put a time limit on their ability to walk? No, you would say, however long it takes for my baby to walk, we're going to stand by until that kid walks—period. The same is true for you. Gain a positive attitude of expectancy.

This is the way you need to be for your life without alcohol and drugs in the picture and live the life that you've dreamt for yourself and your family. Until you make it happen. Period. No Excuses.

Take each one of your items—define it, visualize it, feel it and own it along with your why. Ten-minute sessions morning, noon and night, no excuses! If you miss a session don't worry just pick up where you left off and do it again. You can do this walking, running, sitting, driving, riding your bike, taking a break at work, in the shower... just get started.

Take your list and visualize each goal's attainment. See it, feel it, believe it in advance, then feel the why you want it all the way to your bone marrow! Visualize yourself attaining that goal and then see, feel, smell and hear what it's going to do for you and your family. Do these sessions until you feel those butterflies in your tummy fluttering with excitement and anticipation.

Think of it as telling yourself the truth in advance.

You can use many different processes to hardwire your new life into your subconscious mind. Toward the end of the book you will be given several different resources to complete your life mission.

Remember the BBC/BGC (the Big Boys/Girls Club). It's your time to leave the naysayers, the nonstarters, the ho-hummers behind, set your sights in renewed vision and go get it!

CHAPTER TEN

MIND/BODY DAMAGE, MIND/BODY REPAIR: 30+ PROVEN SOLUTIONS THAT WORK

GETTING YOU ON TRACK AND BEYOND!

· ·

A t the end of chapter 3 we researched, explored and hopefully agreed that alcohol and drugs damage both the mind and body. If the use is prolonged and if the mix of chemicals is just right, for many people permanent damage can occur.

A great amount of research has been done on repairing and getting the body to an even better state than before. A state that will support growth in all areas of recovery and beyond! We have found with a mix of current technologies, nutrition and mental processes depending on the person we can really set ourselves up for amazing personal performances and in many cases life-extending performances.

In the following pages we're going to look at several areas that I and others have found to cover the range of needs for a full recovery and beyond.

Please note that I've put together a full body of information for your knowledge uptake. **Please do not be overwhelmed.** I suggest you read through them all first. Make sure you take the Personal Trigger Points evaluation in this chapter and then from there you should have a good idea of what you will need to focus on to get back on track. From there you will be able to choose the best options that resonate with you the most. Remember, in no way am I saying that you have to utilize each one of the following or do exactly what I did to get results. We are all different individuals with different lives and needs. I recommend you select the components that fit best for yourself and we will help you put together and learn how to utilize them for your own unique personal recovery program.

We're going to put these into four groups.

Physical, Mental, Behavioral and Spiritual. (Although you do not need to have a spiritual aspect to your life in order to achieve sobriety, I personally feel that it has been a cornerstone for me in my journey. I would highly recommend if you are without any kind of faith or spiritual belief that you look for a source of greater good and inspiration outside of yourself to turn to when you need whatever that may be for you.)

Research shows that if you feel good you'll perform well and if you feel bad your chances of performing well drop dramatically. It is for this reason I'm going to start with the physical body.

1. Physical fix
A. Hydration - water consumption and proper levels.

Did you know that 75% of Americans are chronically dehydrated? Next time you catch yourself asking, "Why am I so tired?" it may very well be because your blood, tissues and organs are not getting enough water. Interestingly enough the liver and brain are affected the most by lack of water.

Vasopressin is a hormone which regulates the flow of water into the cells in your body. When this hormone reaches a cell it pushes water through a filtration receptor, so only water gets to it and hydrates the cell. This is critical because without that hydration vital organs begin to fail. Consider this, your blood moving through your body is 90% water, your brain and nerves are 80% water. In a normal day you expel about a gallon of water every 24 hours. Not to mention all the crap we put into our bodies daily that sucks water out of our bodies such as coffee, tea, colas, alcohol, smoking, etc. Wonder what happens to us when we don't replenish that supply? You guessed it, forgetting where you put your keys, forgetting your best friend's sister's name, headaches, low energy, crappy attitude, having trouble doing basic math, starting to think that you're not worthy of a good life... Get it?

Just drinking your required eight to 10 eight-ounce glasses of **pure** water per day alone will make you feel amazingly better. Try it! I guarantee many ailments and issues will disappear right before your very eyes. And one of the most important things you will notice pertaining to sobriety is that you will gain a much better clarity of thinking and your brain will just work better. Put the soda can down and reach for your water!!!

For most of us drinking from our tap is not usually the cleanest option. If you really want to take your personal wellness to the next level you can purchase filters or machines that can do many powerful things to your water in order to make it the best water for your body.

- Remove free radicals, heavy metals, pesticides, chlorine, fluoride and lye from your drinking water.
- Look into Ionizing and alkalizing your water. There will be more on this topic on our website.
- Water is a *macronutrient*, **a chemical element needed in large amounts for normal growth and development.**

You can find out more about the water solutions that we stand behind and more about the body of work on this subject on our website at www.ontrackandbeyond.com.

B. Food consumption – Nutritional needs for recovery and food standards for optimal health and wellness.

We are all aware of the overly talked about diet fads that pop up every month and we think we know about supposed healthy eating but here in America we are sorely lacking in that department. America is one of the fattest most toxic and unhealthy countries in the world! Here we're going to talk about what the body needs to function at the optimal level of health, rejuvenation and maintenance. As a senior-level trainer for the United States Government it should be very telling that we never use fad diets or tricks when it comes to making our men and women the best combat fighting forces in the world. Something to think about...We're going to break this down into the **three major macronutrients**: proteins, carbohydrates and fats. These entries are meant to give you a solid but general overview of what food can do for your body in greatly aiding your recovery and providing a good dietary base to work from.

Proteins contain essential amino acids which are the precursors of neurotransmitters, which are generally lacking in problem drinkers. Additionally proteins are the foundation of our muscle tone and help prevent disease. Research shows us that amino acid in the proper dosage leads to lessened withdrawal symptoms, cravings and stress! Isn't that cool? In the next section we'll talk about supplements and the importance of them. For now please be aware that proteins are found in fish, meat, poultry, beans, grains and dairy products.

Carbohydrates are often considered fuel for brain power and will provide what we call right now power to your muscles and brain. One of the biggest benefits of proper carbs is regulation of your blood sugar level which is critical for recovery, balancing your moods and fueling your energy. Fruits, vegetables, grains, pasta, cereal and legumes fall into this category.

Fats come in many different forms and are often not thought of as a good thing by those who are unfamiliar with good eating habits. Good

fats make it possible for your body to regulate its temperature and are essential to the absorption, transport and use of vitamins like A, D, E and K. Fat is an important energy source as well as essential for brain growth and sustainability. Good fats include the following: avocados, nuts, sunflower seeds, pumpkin seeds, flaxseed oil, olives and olive oil, coconut oil, low sodium nuts, cold-water fish.

Proper fat consumption is not to be overlooked as it is essential for optimal health.

Fiber is an essential part of your eating habits. Fiber helps flush out toxins from our body that build up over time. Fiber also keeps the digestive system healthy and functioning properly. Studies have also shown for every additional 10% grams of fiber there was a decrease in developing heart disease by 14%. Fiber can be found in vegetables, fruits, whole grains, nuts and legumes to name a few.

It is my experience that breaking your meals up throughout your day into smaller more frequent meals is ideal for running a clean and strong motor. Instead of three large meals and eating the biggest one at dinner, try four to six small meals, starting heavier and ending up lighter. Try to consume more carbs and fats in the first half of the day (breakfast and lunch) and finish off the day with a lean protein and veggie/salad at night. This gives your body more time to stay active and burn up those carbs/fats you're eating in the first portion of the day. Also when you eat smaller more frequent meals you train your metabolism to stay running much more consistently without those huge lulls or highs and lows in energy level that come from infrequent eating or enormous meals loaded with sugar and starches that spike your blood sugar and make you crash. Just start experimenting with your portion sizes and try changing meals from three a day to four to six a day. Try something like this:

- Breakfast
- Snack
- Lunch
- Snack
- Dinner
- Small snack (optional)

Lastly there are many great free online resources to help you find and calculate how many calories you should be eating for your body type and your personal body goals. Check them out.

In closing on food consumption and recovery this is another huge body of work. Eating healthy food is such an essential part of feeling good; please do not underestimate its power. If you find yourself struggling to grasp an idea of healthy eating I implore you to get out there and seek help or advice, read books, go online, anything to gain current knowledge on how to eat to stay vital, healthy and fully present in your life. Please remember I am just scratching the surface here on food intake yet I cannot stress to you enough how great its importance is to an awesome and long life. Maybe my next book will be on this food topic! Please visit our website for more info on eating right, www.ontrackandbeyond.com.

C. Supplements – the secret weapon to safely accelerating your recovery and safeguarding yourself from cravings.

Supplements play a major key role in the repair of your body. The right supplements can make or break the ease in which your recovery goes and in the long term will provide nutrients that you just do not get from food today. Food quality in today's world is totally unreliable so I believe supplements to be absolutely essential! I personally wouldn't go a day without my supplements! We will focus in on four key supplements here but know that this is also a whole other huge body of work that can greatly benefit your whole life. For more on this topic please visit our website.

First we'll look at **L-Glutamine**. Glutamine is the most abundant amino acid in the body. It is stored in the skeletal muscle and is released in response to physiological stress. In layman's terms if your life is stressed out you'll be accessing your glutamine stores more, if your body has lots of physical demands placed on it you'll be accessing your glutamine stores.

Glutamine is an essential amino acid, meaning you need this stuff no questions asked. But here's the fun part: Glutamine has been proven to reduce cravings for alcohol and drugs by eliminating the strong desire for sugar and carbohydrates! Additionally, it's shown to reduce anxiety! This was and is a major winner in my book. L-Glutamine has played a huge part in my recovery and helps me through my daily stress. I wouldn't be without it. Please check it out!

Next we'll look at **amino acids**. These are the building blocks needed for your body to work properly. Another essential supplement I would never be without. Amino acids are the building blocks of protein which as discussed earlier is majorly essential. Amino acids are the precursor of neurotransmitters. Again neurotransmitters are responsible for every thought, mood, pain and pleasure sensation that we feel.

Two very important neurotransmitters controlling mood, food and energy are serotonin and dopamine. Serotonin is responsible for our feelings of well-being, peace and mood stability. Dopamine is necessary for mental concentration, alertness, high energy, motivation and sex drive. This also helps to reduce withdrawal symptoms, cravings and stress. Not to mention assisting your muscle development and body tone when you start your fitness program...hint, hint.

One of the reasons that it is necessary to obtain supplements is that serotonin (hugely important) is derived from the amino acid tryptophan. Tryptophan is the least common amino acid in food and is the most difficult to absorb into the brain. This occurs because other amino acids fight with tryptophan for absorption and unfortunately tryptophan loses the battle.

Please know these neurotoxins like caffeine, nicotine and alcohol all decrease proper neurotransmission. If you want to get better faster these should be eliminated or at the very least minimized.

There are now advanced supplements called neuro-nutraceuticals that bridge the gap needed for proper intestinal absorption to regulate neurotransmitter levels. Please people the first solution does not have to be Prozac, Zoloft, Paxil, etc. I would highly recommend you steer clear from these as answers as much as possible! Use them only as a very last resort if you absolutely must.

Omega 3s, 6s, and 9s are often overlooked in even the best of dieting programs. Omegas are essential fatty acids. The brain is made up of about two-thirds fats (lipids). Lipids are the part of the brain that promotes membrane flexibility and strength. This same fat covers the branches of neurons promoting electrical transmission of the brain signals. If that's not enough to make sure we add this to our diet let's include that omegas assist in cardiovascular function, nervous system function, skin health, mood regulation, damaged cell repair and reduction of joint inflammation. Additionally omegas lower cholesterol, improve immune function and also protect against certain types of cancer. I hope it's not a stretch to see how important this can be to your recovery program and beyond.

Multi-vitamins play a huge role in our body's ability to recover quickly and maintain the proper support to our dieting habits providing essential vitamins and minerals we can't make on our own or no longer get in today's food. It can't be overstated that a quality vitamin with a high absorption rate is going to be leaps and bounds better for you because your body will actually take the vitamin in and use it rather than eliminate it before it gets a chance to break down. Vitamins help greatly with dietary imbalances and deficiencies and balance our nutritional needs. This is another one that's a basic building block to a better you. You must not overlook this. I make sure I have mine every day with every meal.

In closing on supplements I highly recommend a daily assortment consisting of all or most of the above. Seek out your local health food store or vitamin shop and ask them questions if needed to find yourself the right supplemental blend to add to your daily routine. You must not be without them for long!!!

D. Physical fitness and wellness.

I can just hear you now saying, "More fitness and wellness talk?" Yup! Believe me the benefits of physical fitness and health and wellness **cannot** be overstated!

We now know that just 20 minutes of cardio three times a week provides enough exercise to ward off chronic disease that otherwise could be present and raises serotonin levels in the brain. Cardiovascular exercise will also help in the removal of toxins that come from stress and provide relief from anxiety, thus making attaining and maintaining sobriety much easier. Physical exercise has literally saved my life more than once and I wish more people could truly understand its importance to a great quality of life!

As a senior combat instructor contracted by the U.S. Government I can tell you that your fitness level is directly related to your ability to have mental clarity. Fitness stimulates various brain chemicals resulting in a much better you. We also know that the more you use your muscles and focus, the more you can use your muscles and focus. Let me just say I'm not sitting here thinking you need to do the latest fad in fitness or become a gym rat by any means. General fitness exercises are fine for developing a healthier mind and body. Just getting outside for a brisk walk is all that may be needed. The Greeks revered the well-proportioned, athletic physique. They considered it a step closer to the otherworldly Spirits and saw the health of the body as inseparable from the health of the mind and soul. I believe this to be true in that it clears and frees your mind so you can get closer to your purpose here on Earth.

The following are just some of the benefits of a fitness lifestyle.

- Enhances mood
- Balances and assists in weight management
- Boost in vitality and energy levels
- Adds spark to your sex drive/life
- Promotes better sleep cycles
- Normalizes metabolism
- Increases self-image
- Provides a mental getaway
- Builds and tones body shape
- Creates vitality/vital life force energy

I could go on forever talking about the benefits of a fitness health and wellness program but I'll spare you. I just hope you get the point of how crucial exercise is for all of us to utilize in daily life. In closing a habit changed from a destructive one to a constructive one and how key this is for sustainable sobriety is often overlooked but this is really super-important and for sure something to pay attention to. We'll talk about this later in greater detail. A healthy body is a healthy mind is a key to success. Go for a walk, hit the gym, the treadmill, hire a personal trainer, take a yoga class, just get started on moving!!!

2. Mental health and optimal functionality
Self-esteem / Self-worth

This I believe is one of the biggest ones. My mentor and teacher Jack Canfield says, "Most human personal problems such as drinking, drugging, abuse of any type, anger, rage—i.e., self-destruction—can be rooted back to low self-esteem."

When your self-esteem is high and can cope with life's problems you can produce miracles in your life because a doubting self doesn't get in the way.

Additionally when your self-esteem is right you will attract the right people and events for even more success than you ever dreamed of.

One of the main themes to understand is that underneath every aspect of who we are there's a purpose, a valuable contribution that we're called to bring to the world. And guess what? You are the only person that can fulfill this purpose. It has your name on it. Know this, there has never been anybody like you before and there will never be anybody like you again. You are totally unique. You say, I believe in it but that's for other people, I'm not meant for anything great. I'm not really that unique. Well DNA and Spirit says different!

If you've lost your groove somewhere in a bottle or a bag well let me assure you you're a marvelous human being just waiting to be set free. If you want to you can get your life back and plenty more. It's your choice!

It is so common in our society to put ourselves down, to talk in a way that's self-deprecating. Talking good about ourselves is uncommon and in fact discouraged in our society. One might think that this type of self-talk would help us, unfortunately it does the opposite.

It's like trying to gain a bright outlook and future by always talking about the bad old days... Never gonna happen! Most who do gain forward momentum lose it because their mind's blueprint stays associated with the bad old days. It's similar to how 85% of lottery winners within five years become broke and accrue more debt than before they won the lotto. They didn't re-associate themselves and train to stay wealthy. They stayed hardwired for poverty or being broke.

You don't have to go around beating yourself up, living in guilt and condemnation. However if you have mental warfare going on in your head because you really don't feel that you're good enough, your self-esteem and self-worth will be cut off at the knees.

A question to ask is, do you really like and love yourself? I mean *really* like and love yourself? Think of somebody or something that you have in your life that you really love and take care of, how do you treat them or it? For most active drinkers or drug abusers this may not be a part of your life right now or you may be so hurt you don't have that vision—YET. You may have to use your imagination, ALL things where imagined first before they where created. Just start somewhere and give it a try.

This may not be the best example but it's food for thought. For me I always kept and still keep my cars in a very clean and well-maintained condition. I am very particular with what is done to my cars and by whom. I am also big on my books I always have and always will take care of my books and am very careful about lending them out. They educate me and others and I value them highly therefore I take care of them.

Another example and definitely one of my life's most important pieces is the relationship with my wife and kids. For some people this seems to be not so popular. But learning to see and treat your spouse and children as the most important people in the world can make all the difference! Once I made an active choice to treat my wife and kids this way, my world changed like I can't describe. If you have the love and support of your family you can become unstoppable. Man once I started to treat myself and my family with complete respect because I love, need and value them, they started loving, needing and—yes—valuing me in return! Yeah baby!!! You reap what you sow!

Do you have something or someone like that, that you really love? Maybe a pet, a spouse, a son or daughter, use this at first to identify the feelings and then ask yourself do you have any similar feelings for yourself?

If your answer is yes, then the secondary question is why are you slowly killing yourself? Nobody who is in their RIGHT mind and truly values themselves would do what you and I did or what your loved one is doing right now. This tells us to look deeper into ourselves. If you do this process it will bring things to the surface for you so you can grow.

If the answer is no, you don't like or love yourself, then you now know you need to work on the self-esteem building exercises to increase the way you feel about yourself.

How confident are you in and with yourself? Do you doubt yourself when you take on a project, when you meet someone, when you make a promise to yourself?

We will be going through some exercises that are going to start the reactivation process of your positive self-esteem. Turning back the clock to a time when you had a positive self-esteem or if you feel you never had one it will rapidly start the process of developing one.

The up-and-coming exercises are going to shake your tree, offer you a modified view of how you think and provide a whole different way of thinking about yourself.

Did you know that a study of children in a U.S. school district showed that 80% of kids in the first grade scored high on a positive self-esteem index, 20% of kids in the fifth grade scored high on positive self-esteem and only 5% of kids in high school scored high on positive self-esteem. This is very telling information which should arm us in how we can mobilize ourselves against this happening to our children.

Another study which I found very interesting asked teachers and parents, who is responsible for their kids' positive self-esteem? The results: 72% of the teachers said the parents were responsible and 78% of the parents said the teachers were responsible. Hmmm... Can you see how this could cause a big problem?

Regardless of what you think parents play the biggest role in their children's forming a positive self-image and self-esteem level. Think about it, we learn how to walk, talk, brush our teeth, eat and drive a car from our parents as well as how to express love, how to feel love, what to value, what to work for, what to stand up for, who to spend time with, how to view ourselves, etc, all this by observing how they do it themselves. When our parents nurture and love us we develop a high and positive self-esteem. When they love us with a hug or a praise of words it says to us "you are worthy, beautiful, smart, loving, kind, good, etc." Basically we learn that we are unconditionally worth everything or worth nothing from how we are treated by our parents.

Just for the record my wife and I are parents to five children and without hesitation my wife and I are 100% responsible for our children's self-esteem. Please allow me to provide clarity here. I am NOT saying that all drinking or drugging can be traced back to parenting. I am a strong believer that anybody who abuses drugs and alcohol or destroys their life through negative behavior has some challenge at the self-esteem, self-worth or self-image level. And these can be rooted in our childhood, but it is identifying this issue and moving past it that will free us from the chains that bind us or did bind us at one time.

Additionally it is in my observation that people become so wrapped up in trying to be like someone else or the person someone else wanted them to be, whether it be social surroundings, peer groups, media, games, etc, they forget that there's a "them" underneath and within everybody else.

Ultimately bringing us back to the passage by Marianne Williamson in the beginning of the book, the line that says *"our deepest fear is not that we are inadequate, our deepest fear is that we are powerful beyond measure."* I believe that so many have such huge fear in actually achieving their best in life that they subconsciously sabotage their success over and over. Why do we do this to ourselves? Is it simply that we've lost sight of our gifts and many don't even believe they have gifts to bring to the world? Yes and this is such a sad place to be. But it is also more than that. People are afraid to reach for the stars because...then what? What will we do then? What will we dream then? What happens when we reach the ceiling? Can we handle it, will we mess it up? Well all I can say is you are serving **no one** by staying small and when you reach for your dreams and do attain them then guess what, you get to make new dreams!!!

The following exercises will develop, reactivate and grow you to a new level of personal being. These are just some of the many processes that you can use to build your self-esteem and self-worth. There are many more resources at our website or if you really want to turbo charge your life come to one of our highly informative and exciting experiential learning events. Visit us at www.ontrackandbeyond.com.

One of my favorite exercises is the **"At my finest and best"** drill. The way you do it is simple and straightforward. Just finish the following statement:

At my finest and best... _____.

For example:
- At my finest and best... I'm a great friend.
- At my finest and best... I cook an excellent steak.
- At my finest and best... I can motivate a student and change their life forever.
- At my finest and best... I'm an excellent worker.
- At my finest and best... I look and feel attractive.
- At my finest and best... I give back to the community.

Do this exercise and come up with a minimum of 50 entries. Ideally you want 100, this exercise will change your mind-set. Do this exercise as a session, put aside 15 to 20 minutes of uninterrupted time just for you. Clear your mind and get started. Don't make it a big deal but the quieter the better. After you've done the exercise, take notice of how you're feeling. Notice how things around you look. Notice any changes in your perception. They may be big or they may be small. Hold any good feeling and know you can have that anytime you want.

This is the process you'll want to follow for most of these exercises unless otherwise stated and please refer to our website for more processes, exercises and resources for your personal success path back to you and beyond.

"The victory log, recharging" process: Next make a list of all your major and minor victories. Write these as sentences that you can read and reread with positive and affirming expression so you can re-create the experience. This will recharge your mental and physical battery so you can take the day's tasks, challenges and people on fully charged, ready for most anything that comes your way knowing that you've conquered XYZ in the past. This is extremely powerful when done right.

Use statements similar to the following, or start with an **"I am"** statement:

- I finished my degree even when times were really hard for our family, and because I followed through we are now better off.
- I continued to keep picking up my workout habits even though I've stopped several times. I know that it will stick one of these times.
- I am a high school graduate.
- I am a victor over the chains of alcohol and drugs.
- I am a loving and supportive husband and father.
- I now consistently make coffee in the morning for my wife and it makes her so happy.

- One of my biggest victories in life is being married to my wife.

Notice that each statement has a reference to **you**, meaning the statement has an I or my in the sentence. Remember this is a drill to build your self-esteem and personal self-worth.

When doing these exercises do them until you start to feel better or until you feel a change inside. This is where the importance of being quiet and alone comes in. It is absolutely key for you to identify with the changes that are happening inside you. Trust me if you do this right those changes will be there!

Another great exercise is the **"warm and fuzzy" drill** as opposed to the "cold and prickly" drill. During this exercise you're going to list all the times either you or someone else made you feel warm, fuzzy and good all over.

These are some of my own personal warm and fuzzy sentences:

- It felt great when I was acknowledged by my Judo teacher when I was 10 years old.
- I remember when my Dad saved me from getting hit by a car that lost its brakes while parked on a hill. It made me feel so good that I had someone who really looked out for me. I remember my Dad holding and hugging me while crying. At that age I didn't quite get how huge that was, but now as a grown man and father, I do! I see him as my hero!
- I remember my wife saying to me in her loving way, "You are the guy for me babe, I love you, but if this is going to work, you need to get your act together." My memory was that this person actually loves me and cares enough about my well-being to be totally honest and straight up with me! That was a new thing and I totally respected it. Holy smokes, even writing this in Starbucks I'm getting all gooey.
- When I flew solo for the first time in a plane, to me it was an

unbelievable and impossible thing that, guess what, I accomplished! Impossible is code for I-am-possible.

- I feel an amazing warmth and love when I walk through the front door at home and my kids come running and attack me with hugs and kisses screaming, "Daddy, Daddy!!!" It's a madhouse of love! I can't compare that feeling to anything else.

Again after you've done this exercise just let it marinate for a few minutes. Associate yourself with the feelings. Get to know exactly what it feels like so next time you'll be able to get there that much faster. Also you'll start to associate these feelings when they happen during other times with those quality things on your "warm and fuzzy" list.

"The power of association" cannot be overestimated. It is a very powerful thing that happens to us every day whether we know it or not and can be used as a power tool to change our state immediately. What do you associate with going to the gym, working out or proper dieting in general? At first look you might say I associate going to the gym with being fit and having a good body. So then are you working out on a consistent basis and do you have a good toned body? If your answer is yes I am fit and have a good toned body, then your association with working out is most likely positive because at the end of the day you work out on a consistent basis and possess a fit toned body. You have a habit that overrides what many people associate with going to the gym, proper dieting or working out, which is usually a negative one. Because their association is a negative one even though they may know the good that could come from going to the gym they come up with all sorts of excuses like one of the following: It's too much of a pain in the ass, the gym is going to be crowded and I'm going to have to wait for a machine, I'm gonna get all sweaty and yucky, I'm going to have to be in that locker room with all those other sweaty naked people—no way!!! I'd rather eat pizza than a salad with chicken, I want those chicken wings with fries rather than broiled fish with lemon and greens, I'd rather smoke a cigarette rather than relieve stress by taking a brisk walk.

As you see the association with an immediate satisfaction that has negative results is stronger than the association that has positive long-term results. Let me challenge you to do a gut check on paper and answer the question, why do you do one thing over another when you clearly know that there's a better, more fulfilling option out there? Is there more immediate pain for you in doing that negative action or is there more immediate pleasure?

Another example of association for me is certain feelings and actions I associated with my mother and how they affect the relationship I have with my wife. Social psychology tells us one of the most influential relationships we have growing up is the one with the opposite-gender parent, meaning if you're a guy the relationship with your mother and if you're a girl the relationship with your father.

I found after learning about the power of associations from a therapist that I brought all kinds of old stuff from mother and our relationship into my marriage. Once these things where identified I could then go to work on changing my associations with imbalanced behaviors thus changing from a reaction to a proper response and then build on that.

The short form on how to change associations is to identify on paper what your association is to a certain person, place or thing. Ask the question, is this aligned with my values or am I reacting from a past association or perceived belief with something similar? Now take the time to write down what you would truly like your response and relationship to be with that person, place or thing and change your association to it. It can be as easy as choosing the carrots over the cookies and in time when you start feeling and looking better because of the choices you made you will then associate feeling and looking good with eating better. Then magically those cookies won't have the same appeal for you anymore. You changed your association with the cookies to a more negative one all the while strengthening the connection to better eating because your actions gave you results. It is now more painful to eat the cookies all the time because you really see and feel the difference in your body and attitude since you've been eating healthy. Simple yet powerful things can come from these adjustments.

Now go out and behave in a consistent manner that supports that new association and belief.

Another great exercise is **"my strengths and good qualities"** drill. This drill is so strong it will have you saying, "I need to be doing more with all my skills and qualities. Why am I wasting something that's so powerful and could be put to good use? You may even catch yourself saying, "A guy or girl with all those skills could be pretty *valuable*..." Now this is leverage! That's what you want these exercises to do! Create a shift in how your mind is "set." This is what is known as a light bulb moment, an aha experience, a paradigm shift.

We do this on a daily basis with military, law enforcement and civilian personnel. We create a massive shift adding a new dimension to their combat that many didn't know existed for themselves and give them tools to use within this new dimension. It's a great thing to watch but an even better humbling feeling to be the agent of such positive change.

In this exercise the sentences would look something like this:

- For some reason I really connect with older folks, I really like talking to them and helping them.
- I have a great visionary mind.
- I have a natural ability to read people.
- One of my great strengths is dogged perseverance.
- I have a special connection with kids.
- My kids and I love each other so much, my strength is that I really foster love into them and continue to look for the good in them.

One additional piece that you may want to add to this exercise is having other people such as caring friends, family and coworkers answer this question for you. Don't be afraid of this part of the exercise if they're your true friend they'll be willing to do it. It takes only five to 10 minutes anyway. Other people who are close to you know more about you than you think and can give you a really great perspective.

Do not do this exercise with your idiot friend Ralph from work who brownnoses you. Do not do this with the girl down the hall that has a crush on you. Use someone whose opinion you really value. Get my point?

This next exercise is a physical task, it's called **"curb it and maintain."** When you complete this exercise and others like it on a consistent basis your self-worth will begin to strengthen at the core level. You'll start gaining a feeling of worth that no one else can take away from you.

It's yours, you're doing it, you're making the choices, you're making changes, you're living with those decisions and that's gratifying. It's all you baby (with a little help).

It is a universal law that order be in place, but let's say if it wasn't a universal law it still would be one of those things that makes damn good sense don't you think? Did you ever get a ride from a friend for the first time whose car was a serious mess? I mean so much stuff like food wrappers, coffee cups, clothes, newspapers, books, CDs, dust, etc, everywhere that you could barely sit down. I don't know about you but I definitely wouldn't ask that person advice on how to be clean and organized in one's life based on that initial impression, are you following me?

Then there's the person who has the older model car (not a collector's if you know what I mean) and it's spotless and runs great. I bet you'll think a different way about him or her.

The point here is not to have a clean car but to suggest that what you have in your environment is a reflection of your conscience and self-worth.

The "curb it and maintain" exercise is the removal of clutter, crap and chaos from our lives. What this means is yes, if your car is a disaster zone clean it up and make it an ideal to keep it clean. If your closet is like a war zone and you haven't been able to dip a toe into it for months, clean it out! If the garage isn't in a way that's a reflection of you, make it a reflection of you!

One of the biggest things that gave me great results and made me so much better as a person was the curbing of actual people in my life that were going nowhere fast, highly toxic and self-absorbed. Having a life free of clutter/junk *is to be free*! Free yourself up to enjoy your life and not be bogged down by your environment or the people in it.

Please remember there are two parts to this exercise *curb and maintain*, sometimes the maintain part can be harder because it's a habit and habits must be formed, so if you fall back on your tasks just pick it up again. And remember to be patient with yourself.

The people thing can be really hard because once they notice you're moving on to bigger better things often they will try and pull you right back down with all sorts of clever tricks. Many times they don't even know that they're doing it but surprisingly many do. Basically people often do not want to see you grow beyond where they are.

Relationships that are majorly less than and we allow to go on in our lives are toxic and a reflection of us and how we feel about ourselves. Remember you are who you become hugely because of the relationships that we keep. Remember the birds of a feather thing. Be aware and stand guard at the door of your life.

The next task is keeping **"objects of your affection"** that are very valuable to you. For me some of them were my first pair of boxing gloves, the martial arts uniform that belonged to my Dad which he passed down to me, my first black belt, a few of the first love notes my wife gave to me, one of the first pieces of art that I did, one of my first guitars and the shirt that I wore when I flew my first solo signed by my instructor and all the pilots in the tower at the time.

These are all objects that we can put in places around our home or our environment where we will see them regularly to remind us that we are worthy and have done great things. When we see these things we

134 YOU'VE BEEN LIED TO...

can stop and take a pause to reflect on what we've done. This is another simple task that has a high value outcome, believe me!

"Neutralizing old tapes" – Old tapes that play over and over in your head from the past can cause major triggering issues and bring on cravings that may push you over the edge to drink/use or just wreak havoc on your day. This was something I struggled with for a long time. But I found two ways that seem to work very well in stopping those old tapes from running through your head. The first is to simply say, "STOP!" Just as in a real conversation if someone were to say "stop" to you, you would probably do just that—stop talking.

This works the same way with your self-talk and old tapes replaying themselves. Say it, scream it, yell it, speak it in your mind over and over, whatever you need to do just do it. I even went so far as to wear a rubber band around my wrist to snap myself with if I had old tapes sneak up on me. This immediately interrupted my pattern and then I would say, "STOP!" Once you've said stop that's when you have to start your new tape playing. Often the bad old tapes will try to run again and default you back to your old ways. Just say "STOP!" again and start up your new empowering video or audio. If you have to force yourself, then force yourself. I know it may feel very awkward in the beginning but believe me it will get easier and be so worth it! Also try to remember that we see things in pictures in our mind so strengthening your words with good pictures will add great power to changing from the old tapes to a new clearer picture that will, with practice, completely replace the old.

The second way you can neutralize old tapes and cravings is to stop what you are doing and notice what is occurring in your body. But the most important part is to then change what you're doing, maybe do 100 sit-ups, 50 pushups, walk around the block, clean up the kitchen or wash the car, you get the idea. This is what I did with the rubber band on my wrist. What you want is an interruption to your system and a lane change. Another quick tip is to change your breathing pattern. Taking deeper breaths intentionally for a period of time no less than 30 seconds can work miracles for you not to mention deep breathing is highly beneficial to your physical body. This in and of itself could do the trick.

Remember at first you may have to do this several times before you get it. Just keep trying. Know that with hard work and determination you can and will be successful.

"Performance Mind Programming" – This tool has to be one of my favorites. I've had the best success with it using it as the controller that brings all my other efforts and practices to use. What do I mean by that? Performance Mind Programming is just that—programming the subconscious mind to perform and direct the conscious mind to act out the program. Think of this as software for the mind and hardware for the body, the software controls your hardware.

Let's say we're talking about the art of replacement where I substitute one behavior for another after defining that the new behavior would truly serve me much better. I won't lie to you, creating a replacement action and writing about it will create only so much movement for you. On its own it won't be enough, you're really going to have to want to make it better and sometimes that old behavior will try and creep back into your life.

Once I started putting the behavior that I wanted in the place of my old behavior in my performance mind program it was crazy because I pretty quickly found myself doing the new behavior like it was the next natural step. I would just take action and sometimes actually question myself later, hey were did that come from? It really works. Think of it as your software upgrading.

Performance Mind Programming is the same component professional athletes use before and during training exercises or key events. It's mental visualization with the rehearsal of the desired new behavior or result. This is so powerful it's unbelievable how well this stuff can work. That's probably why the best of the best use it. Do you know the military aerial acrobatics team the Blue Angels? You know the guys that use five fighter planes traveling 500 miles per hour, three feet apart, to do all kinds of craziness in the air! These guys do this 300 times a year and before each performance they as a team go into a dark room with small model planes in hand and rehearse every move from start to finish along with all the verbal communications.

One might say, well those guys really need to do that because it's super-important that they be on point for every move, and my response to that is, aren't your life and your dreams super-important too? Isn't eliminating the parts of your life that are holding you back from being your best crazy important? Hell yes they are!

How this works is by taking the behaviors, things and places that you want and visualize yourself having them, doing them or being there. Talk to yourself in "I am" statements as discussed earlier, and in every area that you want, see it as clearly as you can in your mind's eye. You'll also want to place your name in the statement. An example would be "I, Hank Hayes, am lean and fit and I eat only fresh organic foods."

There are two key times of day that you will want to do this—just as you're getting out of bed and just before you go to bed. You do it fresh in the morning so it programs your mind for the day. Think of it as the first set of instructions that you'll get in the morning that align with your values and your goals, pretty cool huh? The reason you will do this before you go to sleep is once you're asleep, your conscious negativity and internal doubting Thomas cannot question or argue with the new program. You get six to seven hours of REM sleep with the new program in your head and no one to talk you down. Now that's serious programming, this is why it works so well. Additionally this type of programming should have a 21-day loading phase, meaning you'll continue to do this while living with your negative habit or not. The idea is to the get the programming installed in the mind.

I like to do this while working out, it's called moving meditation performance programming. You can do short visualizations while standing in line somewhere and you don't have to close your eyes. You won't get the same value at the subconscious level but it does significantly help your daily mind-set and the more you do it the better off you are.

In closing on Performance Mind Programming having a recording of this in your own voice with your ideal behaviors and desires installed with a cadence to access the proper brainwave cycles, is the best way to accelerate this process. At our website and live events you can purchase standard recordings or if you like we can customize a morning, evening and anytime recording for you with your desired music in the background.

Our website is www.ontrackandbeyond.com.

"Hypnosis" – Hypnosis is a very powerful tool for change, especially if you want to change as opposed to a person that is forced. Hypnosis of this type is used to relax the mind and to aid in mind-set repair. Some have used the term hypnosis to reference brainwashing, however it may more appropriately be termed as brain cleansing. Most often when a person goes to a trained hypnotherapist, he or she usually is in a state of loss or powerlessness. This person holds the belief that he or she does not have the willpower to make the change(s) on their own. Better said, they have hypnotized themselves into believing they can't change on their own.

Simply put, what hypnosis does is cleanses the mind of the limiting beliefs and directs that person back to the power they had all the time. While you are in a state of hypnosis you are in the state of expanded consciousness or awareness. This state is a place of infinite possibility; this is where the magic happens! It's the therapist's job to help you get there. Remember all hypnosis is self-hypnosis; without the willingness of the subject this mission would most likely fail.

This is another tool that I have personally used and still use with great success.

In closing on hypnosis if you think that hypnosis will work for you, you have a very good chance that it will. No effort that you make is a failure; you're just one step closer to the solution.

"Brainwave optimization" – This was personally a fantastic experience for me and if I were to try and explain it scientifically I would seriously not do it justice as well as probably greatly confuse you. However what I can do is explain it to you in layman's terms as best as I can and share with you what I witnessed myself and observed in others.

Our brains have and operate at certain frequency levels within regions of the brain. When the brain isn't at optimal levels you have an imbalance and a conflict. This is a brain out of harmony with itself, it's in a constant state of tension, making addictions, bad habits and ailments feel right at home.

Through a series of noninvasive sessions where sensors are placed on different locations on your head and using sound patterns the brain balances itself to a state of synchronization and harmony.

It's like front-end alignment for your high-end sports car, but better. Visiting the main headquarters in Arizona was an outstanding experience for me and many others I know as well. The clarity of mind, peace and happiness that I attained during my days in Arizona was nothing short of amazing!

Brain training can be used for just about any ailment or just to enhance performance. This is truly cutting-edge technology. I highly recommend Brain State Technology to take you to the next level and beyond. Contact them directly at http://www.brainstatetech.com/ or get in touch through us.

"Counseling" – One-on-one counseling or small group semi private counseling can be an excellent tool in addition to your recovery program. It can provide a personal focus to you and your challenges alone which is something that you won't get in a large group environment. A good counselor within a few sessions can assist in getting you on the right track and provide the support necessary for you in staying on that track.

To quote the great American football coach Vince Lombardi Jr., "All it takes is one. One great play, one right diet, one right girl or guy." In therapy all it takes is that one right someone saying that one right thing to you and it could change your life forever.

Make sure your counselor or therapist knows exactly what you subscribe to recovery-wise such as if you believe in the disease model and faith healing or not.

One of the most important things in counseling, therapy or group support is that you feel fortified and strengthened from your involvement in the group. This is huge for your growth as a mature, stable, self-actualized individual.

"Self-image" – This one is built and leveraged from your self-esteem. Allow me to explain. Self-esteem is how you feel about yourself. Self-image is how you see yourself and how you believe others see you. Additionally it includes how much you like yourself or how much you think others like you. This also includes the status you feel you have in life.

Your image of yourself has to do with perception. How you see yourself is critical because this will directly affect how you act, how you think and how you act with others. People will generally respond to you in direct proportion to your level of confidence.

Your view of yourself is created by your individual thoughts and beliefs. Your self-image will change radically when you start feeling better about yourself by doing the exercises mentioned in the self-esteem section. There are several things that you can do immediately to boost your self-image, however you're going to have to do the self-esteem exercises to really make that deep long lasting difference.

It can be as simple as making your bed every morning. I know you might be saying that I have done lost my mind with this "make your bed" stuff but it's a simple task with a big payoff. It's about starting your day with order and doing good things for yourself. Try it for a week, I guarantee you'll feel better about yourself.

Purchase some clothes that look good and make you really feel good about yourself. This is an immediate game changer. It's like driving an expensive car. If you ever had the opportunity I'm sure you noticed all the looks you got and perhaps how people treated you a little different. This is the immediate change that new clothes and clothes that fit you really well will do for you.

Modify your personal appearance to the person that you want to be. Be courageous and go get that haircut you always wanted to try. Shave off that beard you've kept for five years, get your teeth cleaned, have a regular manicure, basically polish yourself up and most importantly enjoy it!

Another task that will make a big difference in your self-image is

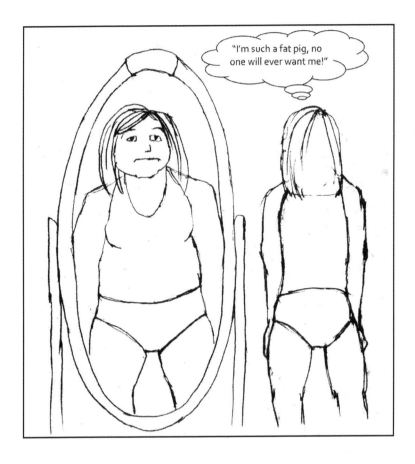

taking care of yourself through fitness. We spoke about this earlier, however I cannot express enough how awesome this will make you feel. Try this drill right now: Think about having the body that you want, the muscle tone, the leanness, the confidence. Close your eyes and visualize that body right now. Stay on that image until you can see it with ease, you relax into what you visualize and you start to feel it...

Okay, did you feel a change in your mind-set? Did a smile cross your face or did you notice a change in the way you feel about the idea of having that body? Now ask yourself this: If just thinking about it does this to how you feel, what would actually having that body do for your self-image?

The last exercise follows the quote **"We are what we think about all day long" and the concept of "law of concentration,"** which states the idea of whatever you think about will grow in your experience. Life success, a positive image and true self-confidence starts with taking purposeful systematic control of the thoughts we allow to occupy our conscious mind.

The most powerful way to gain full control over our conscious mind is utilizing statements that start with "I."

I like myself
I like myself
I like myself

I am attractive
I am attractive
I am attractive

I am successful
I am successful
I am successful

I am responsible

I am responsible

I am responsible

There is a one-on-one relationship with responsibility, control, personal freedom and positive emotions. As well there is a one-on-one relationship with irresponsibility, lack of control, lack of personal freedom and negative emotions. Use this every day with all the positive "I am" statements you can think of.

3. The Art of Behavior

Yes we are going to talk about behavior but no you're not going to hear it pitched in the same old way. It is my goal that by presenting it in a slightly different light you'll see it differently, process it differently and then ultimately use it differently.

We're going to use two scenarios to paint a picture for you. Let's use the job market. At this time it's January 2011 and because of the economy each interview we may go on is very important. You have to "bring it" if you will, otherwise we're back out there looking for opportunities that are very slim.

Imagine that you're an interviewing employer, and in walks a gal with a frumpy look, her shoulders are slumped, her hair is unkempt and she's wearing clothes that look like she slept in them. To boot her attitude rivals Eeyore the donkey's from *Winnie the Pooh*. You can tell she is trying to show a sincere smile and you admit to yourself she does have the job skills but man you're just really not feeling her. All that comes to mind is if this is how she is with me, the all-important interviewer, how is she going to be when she's hired? Probably not any better... NEXT! She will not be scheduled for a second interview.

Next a girl walks in with positive energy; she shows eagerness but not over the top and you can tell she's aware of what's going on around her. She is professionally dressed, seems well put together and has all the skills but most importantly her attitude is great and one that you want to have around. She is scheduled for the next interview. Her attitude affects her behavior which affects the outcome.

The second story is about the guy that has it all and thinks he's entitled. This guy is looking for a collectable that is very rare and hard to find. He eventually locates this collectable and he tries to make an appointment with the owner to see it. But he learns that the owner has plans to leave town for two weeks the very next day, so he gets pushy.

He successfully makes the appointment for that day. The owner is not exactly thrilled with this man's tactics as it is cramping up his schedule; nevertheless he stays with the appointment. Once they meet the prospective buyer broadcasts that "I'm super-special" attitude. But he is not exactly pleased with the dust all over the collectable not taking into consideration the fact that the seller didn't have time to clean it because of the tight schedule he put him in. This overall attitude has now affected the seller to a point that makes him feel very negative and all of a sudden, because this item had belonged to his brother who recently died, he won't sell it to the guy for any amount of money.

This is what we'll call a double loss. Because the prospective buyer didn't get what he so badly wanted and the seller felt pushed around and offended by the guy's attitude, neither of them won anything. Bottom line, this meeting didn't leave the world a better place. This is a simple example of how everything affects everything, big or small, and how attitude affects behavior.

How does this pertain to a sober life? It's straightforward: If you have a good attitude toward your sobriety and your life, you'll behave much better toward others and activities in your life, and likewise others will be affected by your positive energy and they will behave better toward you.

I found that once I truly focused on having a better attitude toward life and stopped behaving like a little spoiled brat, playing the victim role, thinking that I had a disease that made me different from my fellows and acting like the world owed me something, gaining sobriety was so much easier!

Once I transitioned to a TRUE attitude of gratefulness things changed for me dramatically. Happiness doesn't fall on us, happiness is an action!

In the words of Earl Nightingale, "People are as happy as they make up their minds to be. Please let me be clear: I don't want to sound like it is as easy as pie or as counting 1, 2, 3. This will take time, practice and tons of effort. But at the same time don't make it out to be more difficult than it needs to be, thinking it's only attainable to the wealthy or truly special.

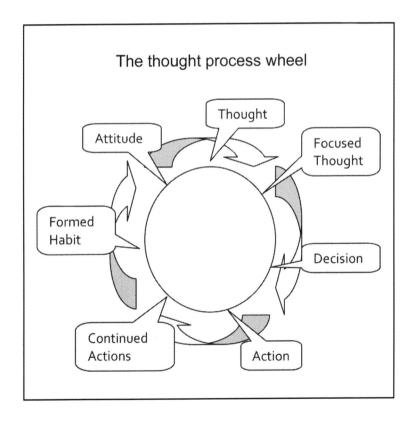

The thought process wheel

Thought

Attitude

Focused Thought

Formed Habit

Decision

Continued Actions

Action

I want to stress to you that attitude is on the front side of positive behaviors and that can change your life forever.

The thought process wheel describes how it all starts as just a thought and then progresses from there to a good result or bad result.

As we look closely at it, we jump in at thoughts at the top. It doesn't matter if it's good or bad; everything starts here as we fix our minds on a thought. Then we move over to focused thoughts. Depending on what sort of thought we have we usually then make some kind of a decision to take action of one kind or another on it. Whether it be skipping the gym or starting that class, you make a decision in your mind which forms into a physical action.

What is meant by continued action is the act of skipping the gym over and over again (bad thing) or going to the classes (good thing, as long as we put that education to use). Bottom line is this is a formed habit which results in a held attitude about your thoughts, decisions, actions and habits.

The following are common thought patterns which are examples of trying to move forward while thinking backward.

- Sustaining a positive attitude through negative assumptions.
- Maintaining a positive happy outlook on life by always assuming the worst.
- Raising your standard of living by lowering your expectations.

If we truly want to have a better life we must believe that we can have that life at the core level, assuming that good things can happen for everyone including us!

"Think better, act better, have and be better."
– Hank Hayes

Now let's talk specifically about behavior and what you do with it. By focusing on this you can change your life.

One of the first things that I found that worked for me very quickly was to look at my behaviors that were rough edged, if you will. In my personality I tend to be very high energy and exuberant but sometimes I feel that I take it over the top, especially when I get excited or upset. So to myself I asked how would I like to act that would be pleasing to me and not so edgy to others. It is the act of removing the unnecessary peaks, both high and low, in my personality and write out what I would rather have my behavior be like.

When I first tried this I didn't know what to expect but the results were so good it told me that if I can get such a good result in just a few days in a major area of my life, what else could I do and what would the rest of my life look like?

It also told me that if I could change a behavior that was a part of my habitual action for my past life I could change other areas of my future life just as easily. This was a major breakthrough for me.

"Just because it's been, doesn't mean it still has to be." *Hank Hayes*

Another activity or practice is *"modeling or acting as if."* This is modeling the behaviors of someone that you really like and respect and you resonate with what they have in their lives. What I mean by modeling is using the words they use, looking at the clothes they wear and how they handle certain situations and using mannerisms similar to theirs.

The first time I did this, to be honest, felt really weird because it was like play acting, however what I noticed was when I acted differently people responded differently to me. This told me that I could immediately affect a change in people around me thus change the outcome of things in my life. WOW! These are simple things you can do **right now** to change your life. It may seem stupid and simple but this truly works.

ACT AS IF UNTIL THE CHANGE STICKS.

There is large body of information and professional help on this topic of study. It's called Cognitive Behavioral Therapy (CBT), where they have a testable measurable method of study and behavior-change therapies. See chapter 11 for resources.

"Overcoming Fear" is another huge body of study. It is said that fear is the number one detractor of people taking action toward the things that would make their lives better. Whether it is fear of rejection, the fear of failure or fear of the unknown any one of these can paralyze us from taking forward-moving action in the direction of our dreams.

The main origin of fear is based on conditioning, mostly connected with destructive criticisms.

The answer in dealing with your fears is to simply analyze them. It is normal to have fears. Everybody does. The strongest most successful people have many fears but the difference is they don't let their fears stop them from taking action. Instead they address the perceived fear, identify what the issue is and break it down into bite-size pieces. This is the first part in gaining courage over your fears and the second part is *taking action*.

Instead of living your life in apprehension, which is the active state of fear adding an unsettled and uneasy state of mind, you can live your life in anticipation and positive expectancy, which is a mental attitude that influences a later response. Tell me which one sounds better to you?

Exercise for *"breaking down fear"*:

Let me say this again, fear is huge! There are volumes of books written on the topic, so please know I am just dipping my toes in on the subject. My opinion is that the main message from most out there regarding the topic of fear is how important it is to acknowledge your fears and then write them down. I know it sounds simple but it can be very empowering! Whether your fear is from the past or of something happening in the future, identifying the fear(s), writing them down and covering all the worst-case scenarios will give you a sense of control and detachment, even if they come true.

If you educate yourself on the topic of your fear you can eliminate the mystery that it may hold for you. Please know that if your fear is borderline phobia then I urge you to seek professional help. Make sure you find a quality doctor who has plenty of experience and who specializes in your issue.

Now that you've identified what is the worst that could happen and you've written this all down, you can realize that you're not going to let any of this happen because you're a go-getter! Now you get to make your list of the results you want to achieve and the actions you are going to take to get to where you want to go. Then focus on achieving those results morning, noon and night!

In addition to this exercise if you find that your fears are a consistent recurring theme, there are plenty of retreats, workshops, camps, events and seminars that directly deal with overcoming fears.

Remember that if fear is where you are in your head and where you want to be seems across the abyss then *action* is the bridge for you to go from fear across and over to your dreams. *Action* is the key!!! Remember you are a *go-getter*!

Another great exercise is a *"personal time study."* One of my favorite mentors Tony Robbins says, "The best study of life is how it is, not how we think it is." For this exercise you'll want to chart how much time you spend in certain areas of your life such as sleeping, working, traveling, playing sports, caring for others, watching TV, going to meetings, eating, abuse-drinking and drugging, working on hobbies, socializing, life planning, educating yourself, spending time with your spouse and your children, etc.

On the following three charts we have different time studies. First is the addicted behavior weeklong time study which is a generalized time base study on my old addicted behaviors as well as feedback from others in their behaviors during my research phase.

Mainstream treatment addiction-free week-long time study

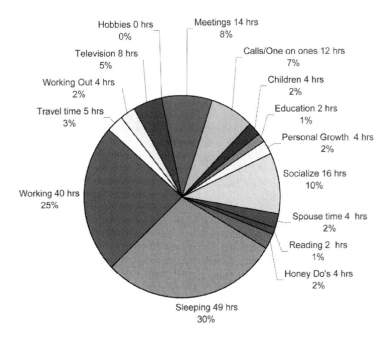

Hobbies 0 hrs
0%

Meetings 14 hrs
8%

Television 8 hrs
5%

Calls/One on ones 12 hrs
7%

Working Out 4 hrs
2%

Children 4 hrs
2%

Travel time 5 hrs
3%

Education 2 hrs
1%

Personal Growth 4 hrs
2%

Socialize 16 hrs
10%

Working 40 hrs
25%

Spouse time 4 hrs
2%

Reading 2 hrs
1%

Honey Do's 4 hrs
2%

Sleeping 49 hrs
30%

The addiction-free weeklong time study again is an assessment of my personal behavior during any given week.

The mainstream addiction-free weeklong time study is from both my behaviors when I was involved in the AA program for over a decade and my current research during question-and-answer sessions on the topic of where do you spend time in key areas in your life.

As you'll see the mainstream program has the individual making a major time commitment to attendance at meetings, one-on-one coffee shop sit-downs, reading the Big Book, working the steps, membership phone time, etc. Okay, that's fine but if you want to get ahead with all the pressures and forces in life pushing on you, you're going to have to make time for personal development, family and health and fitness just to name a few.

Addicted behavior week-long time study

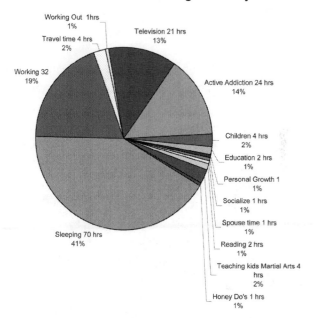

Working Out 1hrs
1%

Travel time 4 hrs
2%

Television 21 hrs
13%

Working 32
19%

Active Addiction 24 hrs
14%

Children 4 hrs
2%

Education 2 hrs
1%

Personal Growth 1
1%

Socialize 1 hrs
1%

Spouse time 1 hrs
1%

Reading 2 hrs
1%

Teaching kids Martial Arts 4
hrs
2%

Honey Do's 1 hrs
1%

Sleeping 70 hrs
41%

Addiction-free week-long time study

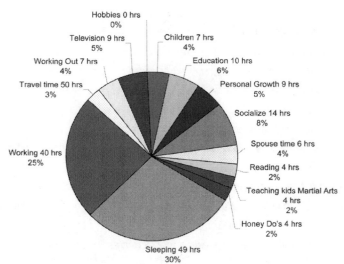

Hobbies 0 hrs
0%

Television 9 hrs
5%

Children 7 hrs
4%

Working Out 7 hrs
4%

Education 10 hrs
6%

Travel time 50 hrs
3%

Personal Growth 9 hrs
5%

Socialize 14 hrs
8%

Working 40 hrs
25%

Spouse time 6 hrs
4%

Reading 4 hrs
2%

Teaching kids Martial Arts
4 hrs
2%

Honey Do's 4 hrs
2%

Sleeping 49 hrs
30%

Doing this exercise is a major eye-opener. By really seeing what you do and where you're spending your time you will subconsciously be driven to make changes in your life even for the most supposed normal or balanced person.

You can go to our website, plug in your own numbers and get your own personal weeklong time study chart; go to www.ontrackandbeyond.com.

The **"art of replacement"** is a major game changer if you take action on it. This is a great follow-up to your personal time study because now you know exactly what you're spending your time on and you can make choices on where to make adjustments.

This is simple and straightforward but you'll have to take charge of your life and make a shift in what you're doing by replacing old destructive actions for constructive ones.

There is only one reason why we do anything. It is for a feeling. We take action because either we believe it's going to make us feel a certain way or it actually does make us feel a certain way, in the end we do it for a feeling.

Please allow me to explain. You buy a suit because it's going to look good on you, which is going to make you feel a certain way about yourself. You wouldn't buy a suit that made you look bad; you'd feel terrible wearing it. You date or marry a certain person because of the way that person makes you feel—better, worthy, cared for, complete, etc. it's a feeling that you get. Healthy people don't date or marry people that make them feel bad.

The same thing applies to your drinking or drugging; you do it because it makes you feel a certain way. However at the time we didn't know the tables would turn on us into a destructive abusive habit. But just like that bad relationship you can get out anytime you want.

You can still get what you were once looking for in that bottle or bag. You can use the art of replacement to fill that need.

Please allow me to provide a few examples from my life which will give you the jump start needed for how you can use replacement to gain healthy fulfillment in your life.

What I found after researching myself was that some of my drinking and drugging was a huge release mechanism to relieve pressure from my life's stresses. What I found out was that stress is built-up energy in my body that needs to come out. So if I used that energy in a positive way I would have lots of endurance. After a while when working out was consistent in my life I had a much better natural balance. A negative energy release valve if you will.

I used constructive working out as the replacement for destructive drinking as a stress relieving tool.

Another replacement activity that I implemented was this: During the old drinking days I felt like I was the big man on campus. Doing this behavior allowed me to go to a place of feeling important which obviously was something I needed. In addition to this feeling I would seek out lower companionship to feel even better about myself. After deep soul-searching and becoming a happily married father of five I finally realized I had all the love and respect that one could ever want or need in life right in my own backyard. Why hadn't I seen or felt it before? It wasn't that my family didn't give it to me. It was because I wouldn't allow myself to feel it the way I needed to. All I did was switch my perspective by writing down over and over and over how important I am to my wife and family and how very important being a fully engaged dad is. I wrote and wrote these things down until I could truly feel and wrap my head around just how important I am to my little girls, my sons, my wife. I wrote until I had tears in my eyes! I honestly felt it deep in my heart at that point. Talk about an emotional anchor. From then on the exercise got easier and easier to do whenever I needed it. This is the art of replacement.

In setting up your replacement program remember it's the feeling that you're after just like the above examples. This is a SUPER-powerful tool that thousands of people who got sober on their own have used and sometimes this is all they needed to make the change to 100% sober.

4. Handling cravings and your reward system

This is where I'd like to introduce the third key:

Personal Trigger Points (PTP)

Your personal trigger points are the people, places and things that set you off or trigger your temper. By knowing where not to be and who not to be with you are ahead of the game. Another way of putting this is being aware of your points of pain. For me in the beginning I had to be careful with conversations with my mother, in the past I had given her the ability to push every one of my buttons. I had to learn how to handle myself around her because I couldn't wait for her to change anymore. I was going to have to take control of these situations for myself.

Triggers were also something that I wasn't able to totally escape. I suspect that you or your loved one might have the same issue.

Triggers are things that set you off and can be just about anything that you associate with drinking, drugging or that destructive habit.

Only you know what those triggers are for you. But in some cases you may not yet be aware of what those triggers are because you haven't searched your mind or your behaviors well enough yet.

Something that I did at motivational speaker and founder of the SMART Recovery Program Tom Horvath's place in San Diego, California, was to take a basic test, which built a current habit and actions profile for me. I answered basic questions about my habits, how I felt about certain things, how money issues affected me, what things pissed me off, what my triggers were or what type of things would happen before I would drink.

The graph data sheet that was produced was another major eye-opener. I could see on paper where, when and with whom I was upset, what would set me off and what my cycles were, etc.

This is way crazy-heavy in gaining yard steps toward your freedom and one of the major gems of this book. This is where your solution lies. You first must know what your deeper core issues are so you can know what to get help with. This in many cases is half the battle.

I have since created a program that produces a similar graph as seen on the following chart. You can access this for your own assessment via our website at www.ontrackandbeyond.com.

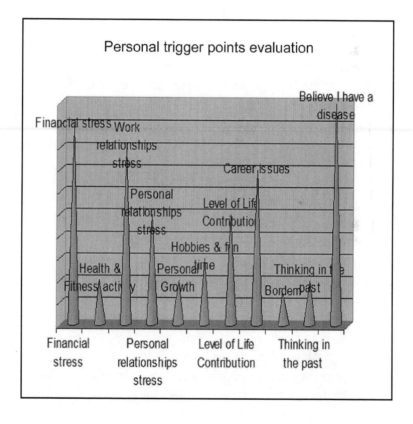

Personal trigger points evaluation

Once you know what those triggers are you can handle yourself much better by:

A) Avoiding that trigger altogether

B) Building a positive association with that trigger, representing change for what that trigger means to you. An example of this may be that you used to go to the bar with a friend after the gym a lot or maybe you often had some type of pick-me-up before you went to the gym. The gym should be a positive thing in your life, so start changing your activities before and after the gym to simple yet positive ones such as stretching while listening to a meditative CD or picking up a smoothie at the juice bar with a friend afterward, thus after time and practice, changing your trigger association.

C) Learn different ways to handle that trigger which we'll cover next in cravings. One thing that helped me when it got tough was thinking about the fact that if one man or woman has done this before then I can do it too! No one said that it would be easy but if I did it and hundreds of thousands of other people have done it...so can you!!!

Please remember there was once a time I thought that I could never get off the sauce but I did. I know you can too!!!

In dealing with cravings there are many ways you can do this. Earlier we talked about supplements that can help out tremendously with your cravings. You can also seek out an evaluation from your doctor about Naltrexone, which is a receptor antagonist; in other words it's a medication that curbs cravings for alcohol and drug dependence. I've never personally tried it, however my research and personal feedback suggests it could work well. However like I said earlier in the book please be so careful when dealing with any pharmaceuticals. I would highly recommend trying this only as a last resort.

Another technique I got from Horvath is what his staff referred to as riding the wave. It was a great way of describing how cravings can come on and hit you. Sometimes they come in sets, sometimes they come in the form of a big crashing wave, sometimes they come in the form of a building tide and at times they don't show themselves for long periods of time then come in multiple sets one after another.

The idea here is learning to ride the wave out and know it will go away—not to give in to it. Please let me be clear: This can sometimes seem like the hardest thing in the world at the time and you can feel as if you're going to die if you don't drink or use. But you will not die!!! It will be hard yes. Maybe the hardest thing you've taken on but know that you can do it and I and hundreds of thousands of people are behind you.

The key is in knowing and trusting it will go away and that you will not die. But the best part is every time you successfully make it through a craving you are moving toward that better life strengthening the good association and moving away from that old life, making the bad association weaker simply by not fueling it.

This brings us to your reward system. It's funny that so many people don't feel okay rewarding themselves after achieving a success in such an area; for some reason, they don't feel deserving. I challenge that, I believe there is no better place and time to reward yourself, this is a huge accomplishment and should be rewarded.

Just make sure you don't reward yourself with a drink or drug. Hey don't laugh it's been done by many, including myself.

In creating your reward system you can use milestones if you like or give yourself a reward every time you successfully make it through a craving, or you can do both. You're in charge of your life, so you make the reward system work for you. Reward yourself with a coffee; a dessert; a massage; a dinner out with your husband/wife; a day skiing with your kids; a weekend away; a trip to home depot, the mall, or the movies; that pair of shoes you've had your eye on. The point is creating a healthy reward system that becomes part of your life. This changes your focus/mind-set and will be a huge part in building the new you, the clean and sober you and much, much more.

The next behavior I would like to discuss is your *"financial life"*.

I am not by any means a financial advisor, so I won't get into a detailed course of action here. I'll leave that for the experts. But I do want to stress to you how important and freeing financial security can be for you and your life if you get control of your financial affairs and have them working for you rather than working against you! There are several excellent experts that can help you get on track very quickly. We have them listed on our website but the three that I'll recommend here and that helped me the most are Suze Orman, David Bach and Dave Ramsey. guys helped to shed light on my financial state, kicked me in the butt and guided me through the repairs. I feel so much more at ease within myself and with life in general knowing what I'm working with and how strategically with my plan can handle anything that may arise. Such a wonderful feeling!

One more thought on this money topic. Money is important! You always hear people say how money really is not what's truly important in life and we shouldn't really focus on it, yes that is true in a very deep way. But there is a flip side to that. Try living without any money to cover your bills, food for your family, your kid's clothes, your house, your car, anything fun, etc. See how unimportant it is then. Try going to your mortgage banker, the gas company, the car dealer or Wal-Mart and saying, "Hey can I get a pass? I'm a good person who loves my family, goes to church, donates blood and I'm clean and sober, so can I skip my payment this month?" Like that's ever gonna happen! Did you know that financial issues/problems are the number one reason for divorce in America today? You cannot convince me that money is not important to life!

Living in a constant money crunch or from paycheck to paycheck is no way to keep the stress level low in your sober life. Please do yourself a favor and take it seriously enough to better your finances, to make more money, to be more organized and to stay committed to the importance of financial balance.

Please do this exercise to help get you started with your financial freedom plan. To take it further check out our website for more resources.

30-day question: Write out how your life would look and feel if for the next 30 days you had all your finances handled. Make your list full of details so you can create those positive vibes in your body associating yourself with financial freedom in your life. Write down what you

would do, how you would take your wife out to dinner and not have to worry about the credit card going through. How you would finally purchase new brakes for the car that you've been putting off for way too long. Get your daughter the pretty pink ballet shoes she's been wanting for two years. Take your son to the big sports game you've always wanted to see with him and create priceless memories! You get the idea. Then make a plan of action and do it!

5. Spirituality

"Your spiritual element to your sober life and beyond" – I first want to mention that you do not have to have a spiritual side to your recovery program whatsoever if that doesn't resonate with you. It is not a requirement in gaining sobriety but having said that, spirituality is a big part of my life as a whole and also a big part of my sober life. I cannot say enough about the use of my spiritual connection and the power of it.

Having said that there are many different religious and spiritual beliefs and it is not my place to say what is right for you. But what I will provide here is what I believe to be a universal idea for anyone to be able to grasp. Later in the book I outline what my program of recovery has been and in that are some specific religious and spiritual practices and paths.

I found this paragraph the moment after I prayed for the right words to express a universal message.

"By embracing the diversity in all of life, we recognize the divine presence in all beings. We seek to remember that we, along with all creatures, are expressions of 'Spirit' and that love is always the deepest truth between us." Universal Spirit Center

In meditating on this statement I hope it will bring you to a different level of awareness and consciousness getting you closer to the true you, after all isn't that what we're after?

CHAPTER ELEVEN

OVER 50 NON-MAINSTREAM RESOURCES FOR YOU TO USE TO GET YOUR LIFE BACK ON TRACK

· ·

There are so many ways to get yourself or your loved one into the right environment to get better. Some people will need help at a facility, some can do it with the help of a few books and some will just make that decision to change their lives for the better.

The following is a roster of resources that I am personally familiar with. These are books, websites, recovery facilities and therapist practices. What you'll find they all have in common is that very few if any at all talk about having a disease.

These are not in any particular order. I've included a little brief along with some of them, and others I haven't. Just remember you are responsible for your life—not the government, not your spouse, not a sponsor, not me, not your priest, nobody but you! Ask for help when needed, accept help when offered but be sure to do your own homework to find what works best for you.

Please read through the following section and do not underestimate the power in gaining knowledge from others who have come before us and what they have found out about the lies we've been told and the solutions that hundreds of thousands of people have found. This social proof may be the lynchpin that helps in sealing your paradigm shift to create a better you.

Okay, here we go.

The Bio Sanctuary at Shangri-La Environmental Health Institute

The Bio Sanctuary at Shangri-La clinic is a scientifically supported comprehensive treatment center providing functional medicine that relieves you of the symptoms you suffer by discovering and treating the CAUSE and CURES of your addiction to prescribed/pushed drugs and/or alcohol, reclaiming your life from the torment of drugs while providing sustainable green mental health for a lifetime! There is an underlying physical condition causing your adverse mental health symptoms and addiction. Heal the root cause and both the symptoms and addiction go away, liberating you from the prison of chemical toxic abuse to the body and mind.

Genita Petralli, HHP, NC, MH, is the director of the medical program at the facilities in Malibu, California, and Costa Rica. This woman is a wealth of knowledge when it comes to the body and what causes addiction habits in her book *Alcoholism: The Cause & the Cure*. She does a fantastic job of helping you understand what occurs in the body at the biochemical level and how to lose the compulsive desire to drink in seven to 10 days. I am a big fan of Petralli's work and greatly enjoyed her book. Her work can definitely take your life to the next level of health. Access to Petralli and her team can be found at:

Genita Petralli HHP, NC, MH
Medical Director
Shangri-La Green Mental Health & Addiction Recovery Center
US: (831) 440.8686 ~ Costa Rica: 8750-2492
www.BioSanctuary.com
www.the101program.com
www.greenmentalhealthcare.com

Passages Malibu Rehab Center

These guys are a father and son team whose journey started when Chris Prentiss was searching for help for his son Pax who at the time had a major addiction challenge going on. Chris found what most of us have, the same old story from rehab to rehab. Chris and his son Pax did exactly what I did for myself and put together their own PRP (personal recovery program) and from that they have created a world-class program in which thousands of people have found lasting recovery. In the following brief I'll include a piece from the Passages Malibu website and their book *The Alcoholism and Addiction Cure*.

"We're a father and son team, along with a team of skilled therapists, who specialize in offering effective rehabilitation treatment to completely cure your addiction. Our treatment program is not like any other in the world for many reasons.

We are not 12-step based, we won't place you in groups all day that preach the disease concept of addiction, and place degrading labels on you like addict or alcoholic. You're better than that, and along with being free from addiction; you deserve to be free of the labels as well. For most of you that will be refreshing to hear, for others, maybe not, perhaps you still want to wear the label of addict and alcoholic even after you're sober, such as they do in the 12-step programs, if this is the case, then we may not be right for you. If you are ready to lose the identity of addict or alcoholic, achieve lasting sobriety, and live a life of health and happiness, then we are right for you. If this resonates with you, then please read our philosophy and learn more about our rehab.

"Addiction to drugs and alcohol is a symptom, not a cause, and not a disease. Addiction is triggered by either mental or physical pain; the drugs and alcohol are what you do to cope with it. To heal your addiction permanently, you must first go to the underlying cause, and heal it; then the addiction will cease to exist. In essence, you will have removed the thorn, the pain will subside, and so will the need for drugs and alcohol.

"Many of the underlying causes that trigger addiction, and which we regularly heal at Passages are low self-esteem, depression, anxiety, panic attacks, loss of loved ones, trauma, molestation, headaches, insomnia, many sorts of physical pain, chemical imbalance, neurotransmitter imbalance, weak drive, ADD, lack of purpose, and family turmoil. There are many more underlying causes that we help our clients discover and heal, but those are some of the most common. Its underlying problems like these that drive people to use drugs and alcohol, heal those and you have just accomplished a major component in getting sober permanently.

"Underlying issues are the real causes of addiction, not a disease, and as such, are very important to heal.

"We have treated thousands of clients at Passages and they tell us similar stories about why they are using, it always comes down to the pain, pain of the past, pain of the present, pain of something, and that pain causes them to seek comfort with drugs and alcohol. After hearing the life stories of so many people, it becomes clear what causes addiction. You really can't miss it. It amazes us that other treatment centers have not figured this out yet, as they still choose to pin addiction on a disease.

"It's true, we have found the missing link, which is to heal the underlying conditions, and through our discovery, we have saved the lives of thousands of people, this method of treatment is the wave of the future, step into it and make it the present, give us an opportunity to show you how skilled we are at what we do, it will be a decision you will be forever grateful you made. Our doors are open, and we honor the opportunity to work with you. Your life is waiting, so *make this moment count!*"

Wow, these guys really have an awesome total-package program. Their facility would definitely be one that I would consider for myself or someone that I love.

Chris and Pax Prentiss can be reached at
www.passagesmalibu.com/ 866-850-6673
www.passagesventura.com/ 866-571-6014

Rational Recovery

Jack Trimpey is the founder of Rational Recovery and is one of the pioneers in the alternative non-mainstream or AA 12-step work. Trimpey and Rational Recovery are well respected in the alternative-treatment community but more importantly thousands of people have been able to acquire life-lasting sobriety using some or all of the Rational Recovery methods.

The following was submitted to me directly from Trimpey upon request for a brief description of what Rational Recovery is about.

"Rational Recovery®: Alternative to Addiction

"Many people would rather remain addicted to alcohol, drugs, food, porn, or gambling because they reject the lifestyle offered by recovery groups and addiction treatment. Here's the key to independent recovery!

"In Rational Recovery®, you will simply quit your addiction, using a simple thinking skill called Addictive Voice Recognition Technique (AVRT®). You already use AVRT® in your daily life, such as when you catch yourself deciding to do something stupid or immoral. In AVRT®, ideas of self-intoxication are called the Addictive Voice, which is identified as the sole cause of addiction.

Addiction is not a disease but a natural function of a healthy human body; health and survival are intimately connected with deep pleasure, such as in eating, sex, and in a comfort zone essential to life. Hedonic drugs are synthetic, however, producing far more pleasure than eating, breathing, sex, or physical safety. Therefore, the drive to repeat the buzz of alcohol and other drugs is greater than all other biological drives. I have named that super-drive of addictive desire the Beast®. You can hear your Beast® talk in your thoughts, 'You can handle a few drinks or hits now and then if you're just careful; besides getting high is one of the few real pleasures in life; how could you celebrate life or have any fun without getting loaded from time to time...' That endless chatter, along with mental images of the high life, are the Addictive Voice: any thinking that supports or suggests the possible future use of alcohol or other drugs.

"Forget about one-day-at-a-time sobriety, trying to end each day 'sober,' while leaving the option to have 'relapses' whenever you really feel like it. Tentative sobriety creates lifelong indecision about drinking/using, leaving the door open for relapses, downfalls, and chronic addiction. Worse, is addict-identity—feeling defective, marked for self-destruction unless pursuing self-improvement or relying upon outside support, guidance, and supervision such as in recovery groups. Stick with your own beliefs and values—only they can help you.

"In AVRT-based recovery, you will simply quit the use of alcohol and other hedonic (pleasure-producing) drugs—for life. To accomplish this with certainty, you will establish a Big Plan, a one-time decision to abstain from alcohol and other drugs under all conditions, as in, 'I will never drink/use again.' Strangely, the idea of such a final end to your addiction produces anxiety, as if always being in your right mind will make your life boring, hollow, and meaningless, as though the sun has dimmed to mourn your loss.

"This emotional error, wrongly called 'dry-drunk,' governs the lives of addicted people, making them extremely vulnerable to the idea of one-day-at-a-time sobriety.

"AVRT® is recovery with an attitude, a kick-ass attitude in which you seize control, face down the Beast®, and walk away from your long-standing addiction in one, fell swoop, without groups, shrinks, and rehabs. Try to imagine, right now, how it would feel to know (not just hope) your addiction is history, over, nada, kaput. Of course your enemy, the Beast®, predicts hell on Earth, but you aren't an animal; you're a human being with an eye to the future. Imagine the relief of knowing your struggle is finally over! We call this triumphant feeling the Abstinence Commitment Effect (ACE)."

Most people figure out about AVRT on their own, as I did, but you would be wise to investigate AVRT-based recovery at the Rational Recovery website, rational.org, and especially in the new book, *The Art of AVRT.* You can regain your freedom and dignity now by learning AVRT and return to your better self in less than a week!

Jack and his team can be reached at:

Rational Recovery

Box 800

Lotus, Ca 95651

530-621-2667

530-621-4374

www.rational.org

Practical Recovery

This facility is owned by Dr. Tom Horvath. I personally attended his facility when I was still mixed in with AA and 12-step recovery and I found what was provided by his staff really great information. The problem I believe, which has been said by others, with mixing the idea that you have a disease with a solution that is based in a non-disease model will only result in a confused person trying to recover with two very different sets of instructions.

This is exactly what happened to me and when I brought back my newfound information to my supposed friends in AA I was shot down like a deer in Pennsylvania on the first day of hunting. I was left with a feeling of low self-worth and sense that most people in the rooms especially the older members where shunning me out.

When I reached out to Tom and informed him that I was writing this book he was thrilled and was more than happy to contribute. Below is information on Practical Recovery.

"Practical Recovery is a comprehensive, self-empowering (non-12-step, non-disease) addiction treatment system headquartered in La Jolla (San Diego), California. Services include detox, rehab, sober living, and office-based services.

"Practical Recovery aims to help clients address their addiction and related problems by developing realistic solutions that honor the client's unique situation, values and beliefs. In the development of a unique treatment plan there are six primary focuses: motivation, craving, problem solving, relationships, lifestyle balance, and living with higher purpose. For younger adults there may also be a focus on basic life skills.

"The core service is individual sessions. A unique feature of the Practical Recovery approach is that as clients (or residents) get to know the members of the multidisciplinary team, the client decides which ones to continue with, and at what frequency. In time a treatment team just for that client is established. Although clients are free to attend support groups, many elect not to. Those who attend usually attend SMART Recovery (www.smartrecovery.org).

"We know the ingredients you'll need to be successful: self-control, a sense of purpose, solid problem-solving and emotional management skills, good health habits, productive activities and meaningful relationships. Our multidisciplinary staff will work with you, not against you, to accomplish these goals.

"To be most time-effective and specific to your situation, your schedule and our services are customized just for you. Practical Recovery is the leader in collaborative addiction treatment. We collaborate with our clients as well as their partners and family, including them to enhance the social support available for recovery.

"But why collaborate with someone (an 'addict' or 'alcoholic') who makes very bad decisions? Don't they need to be told what to do? No! Recovery is best supported by engaging motivations that are deeper than addiction. Confrontation and giving orders might work briefly. Cooperation is much more effective long term. Our innovative approach to alcohol and addiction treatment, and treatment for activity addictions such as gambling or video games, is non-12-step and non-disease model.

Practical Recovery is a boutique practice serving clients with high

168 YOU'VE BEEN LIED TO...

standards. Many addiction treatment facilities place business first, and practice second. Business is easier and more profitable with fixed lengths of stay, one-size-fits-all, group-oriented programs, and under-qualified, low-paid staff as the primary service providers, but the quality of care suffers. We are owned and operated by psychologists and other health professionals. We know how to place clinical care first. Addiction is a practical problem requiring practical solutions. Every road to recovery is different.

"Practical Recovery provides extraordinary value. After you have identified facilities of interest to you, call us for a point-by-point comparison. Our operational excellence allows us to keep our costs low. We have long-standing referral sources, excellent word-of-mouth advertising, and a highly efficient clinical operation. Traditional addiction treatment providers are often unaware of the alternative addiction treatment we offer. But now, you know you have choices!

"Practical Recovery was founded in 1985 by Dr. Tom Horvath, author of *Sex, Drugs, Gambling & Chocolate: A Workbook for Overcoming Addictions*, President (1995-2008; 2009 to present) of SMART Recovery (smartrecovery.org) and President 1999-2000 of the American Psychological Association's Division on Addictions (apa.org, Division 50), the world's largest organization of addiction psychologists.

"We are very different than traditional alcohol and addiction treatment. Be prepared to think about recovery in radically new ways. It's not too late to be happy!"

Tom is another On Track and Beyond top recommendation.

Practical Recovery
8950 Villa La Jolla Drive, #B214
La Jolla, CA 92037
800-977-6110
858-453-4777
FAX 455-0141
www.practicalrecovery.com
info@practicalrecovery.com

St. Gregory Retreat Center

In doing my research a name that came up often in the non-mainstream world of addiction recovery was Stanton Peele, PhD, JD. Peele, a licensed psychologist, has written dozens and dozens of books. The program at St. Gregory's has much of its foundation based on Peele's work. On their website they do a fantastic job of explaining addiction habits and their recovery program. This is a beautiful facility located in the Midwest away from distractions. I would put this high on my recommendation list for myself or a loved one.

The following was taken from their website.

"The St. Gregory Retreat Center is unlike conventional drug and alcohol treatment centers or alcoholism treatment programs that require attendance at Alcoholics Anonymous Meetings (AA Meetings), and Narcotics Anonymous Meetings™ (NA Meetings™). The St. Gregory Retreat Center has developed and implemented the Life Process Model© of addiction recovery.

"We do not believe, nor does research support the idea that an individual is powerless and addicted forever. We are an empowerment-based recovery program that focuses not just on how to 'not drink or drug,' but what factors are driving those behaviors and dependencies in the first place and how to change them. We believe that people can change their lives for the better and that the term 'addiction' is a better definition of where you are stuck than who you are. The Life Process Model© is comprised of behavior modification training, life-skills exercises, and Cognitive Behavior Training (CBT) in a format not available through any other program in America. Most programs (97%) utilize a 12-step/disease methodology putting control over one's recovery in the hands of a doctor or group requiring a lifetime of Alcoholics Anonymous (AA) or Narcotics Anonymous (NA) meetings. The techniques used in our program are based on decades of research and have proven to be vastly more successful than traditional approaches.

"The Life Process Program© was developed in 1991 by pioneering psychologist Dr. Stanton Peele. Dr. Peele was one of the first researchers to identify and develop a non-disease model for addiction recovery. This is why the St. Gregory's residential drug treatment center is different. The key to reversing the dependency cycle is to provide the tools necessary for an individual to learn new life skills and behavior modification utilizing state-of-the art Cognitive Behavior Training (CBT). Today, as Dr. Peele says, 'The Life Process Program© has become one of the most advanced addiction recovery programs in the U.S.'"

The team St. Gregory's can be reached at:

www.stgregoryctr.com

888.848.9054

Malibu Horizon

Malibu Horizon is a non-12-step recovery program that subscribes to the disease model. I felt like including them as an option for readers who believe in the disease model but do not want 12-step or AA.

The following is from their website:

"Malibu Horizon is the only non 12 step, disease model, therapy based program in the world. There may be other non 12 step programs out there however; we are the only one who believes that addiction is a chronic medical condition.

"Malibu Horizon is different from any other program. We specialize in alcoholism, opiate, benzodiazepine addiction with an emphasis on depression, anxiety, coping and communication skills as well as learning boundaries with others.

"We differ from other programs, because we approach addiction as a brain disease. Our state-of-science, non 12 step, medical model of treatment can best be described as a multi-dimensional approach to drug alcohol treatment. We treat the entire patient, including any underlying conditions."

The contact information for Malibu Horizon is:

www.malibuhorizon.com

877-338-6964

The Saint Jude Retreats

I have had personal experience with the team at the Saint Jude facility and would recommend them as an excellent solution to consider if you're fairly stable with yourself and your sobriety. The staff is on point and they have a solid program.

The following is from the Saint Jude website:

"The Jude Thaddeus Program is social and educational program to help people to permanently overcome their substance use problems. The Jude Thaddeus Program can also assist people in overcoming the emotional problems that typically go hand-in-hand with substance use problems; such as anxiety, depression, anger, general irritability and negativity.

"The Jude Thaddeus Program is the only program that continuously evolves based on measuring program results and ongoing research. And the Jude Thaddeus Program is the only program that provides you with a lifelong solution and the power to build the life you want. There are no judgments, no manipulations, no controlling rhetoric; just common sense solutions delivered with the utmost kindness and respect.

"The key to the Jude Thaddeus Program's success is first providing substance users with the absolute truth about their problem: that there is no disease that has rendered them incapable of making the choice not to use alcohol and drugs, and that they can and will be able to regain complete control over their life. From the very first moment that a guest arrives at one of our beautiful retreat houses, they are treated with the utmost kindness and respect. For their first week in the program, the primary focus is dispelling the myths surrounding 'addiction' and 'alcoholism.' As our entire American culture has promulgated the myth of powerlessness and disease, this is a most crucial phase of the program. In order to be successful, people must first begin to believe that they do have the power to change.

"We teaching our guests the need for personal responsibility for their actions, rather than making excuses for poor behavior and choices, is the cornerstone to rebuilding their lives. A disease or dependency is by its very nature out of a person's control. This is simply not the case with substance abuse. Substance abusers make the choice to abuse alcohol and drugs. Choice is a behavior, not a disease."

The team at St. Jude can be reached at:

www.soberforever.net

888-424-2626

The following are website resources that will assist and support you in your search for information on non-mainstream alcohol abuse, addiction data and recovery solutions.

www.baldwinresearch.com
A drug addiction and alcoholism independent research organization

www.peele.net
The Stanton Peele Addiction Website

www.spectrum.niaaa.nih.gov
National Institute on Alcohol Abuse and Alcoholism
www.ccfaa.com
Canadian Centre for Abuse Awareness

www.store.unexplainable.net
Brain Frequency Recording

www.habitbustingsystem.com
Lee Milteer Habit Busting: A 21-Day Program to Break Any Habit

www.hamsnetwork.org
HAMS: Harm Reduction for Alcohol

www.rightrecoveryforyou.com
Addiction recovery solution and service

www.orange-papers.org/orange-effectiveness.html
The Effectiveness of the Twelve-Step Treatment

www.the101program.com/about_book.html
Alcoholism Treatment Program and Alcohol Addiction Treatment Book

www.assistedrecovery.com/index.htm
Evidence-based, non-12 Step Alcoholism & Opiate drug recovery
Treatment utilizing Naltrexone, Campral & Suboxone

www.alcoholism.about.com/od/non/Non_Step_Support_Groups.htm

Non-Step Support Groups

www.smartrecovery.org
SMART Recovery® | Self Help for Alcoholism & Addiction

www.selfhelpmagazine.com/article/AA-alternatives
Alternative Support Programs (Non-AA) | Articles

www.sossobriety.org
drug - alcohol - addiction - SOS-Save Our Selves - Non 12 Step

www.howdoigetmydaughteroffdrugs.com/2010/04/06/non-religious-
alternative-to-alcoholics-anonymous-and-other-12-step-programs/

NON religious Alternative To Alcoholics Anonymous and other 12 step programs : How Do I Get My Daughter Off Drugs

www.non12.com
Science-based, Medical Model for Addiction Treatment - An Alternative to 12 Steps

www.apositivealternative.com
An Alternative to AA and 12-Step Oriented Treatment Programs

These next three organizations are more than just websites; they provide support with either online meetings or live meetings as well as support documentation.

www.womenforsobriety.org
Women For Sobriety, Inc. is a nonprofit organization dedicated to helping women overcome alcoholism and other addictions. Their New Life program is based upon a Thirteen Statement Program of positivity that encourages emotional and spiritual growth. The website provides additional information about the group, the 13 statements of the program, and links to find groups in your area.

www.lowselfhelpsystems.org
Abraham Low's Self-Help Systems is a self-help mental health program based on the work of its founder, the late neuropsychiatrist Abraham A. Low, MD. Recovery, Inc. offers its members a free method to regain and maintain their mental health and the program is designed to work in conjunction with professional mental health services. The website provides information and background about the group, links to resources for group members and professionals, forum boards for discussions/support, and a directory of the more than 700 group meetings in the U.S. and several other countries.

www.lifering.org
LifeRing is a network of support groups for people who want to be free of alcohol and addictive drugs. They are a group for people who have learned through experience that the only solution that works is to abstain completely. They see the power to get clean and sober inside each person. Through the positive reinforcement of the group process, that power becomes dominant in each person and enables them to lead clean and sober lives. The website provides information about the group, including frequently asked questions, publications, an online forum area for support and links to local meetings.

The following are books I recommend that I have read and/or are familiar with. A few are ones I came upon during my writing of this book which looked highly informative on the subject of recovery and health and wellness.

Diseasing of America: How We Allowed Recovery Zealots and the Treatment Industry to Convince Us We Are Out of Control
By Stanton Peele

The Alcoholism and Addiction Cure: A Holistic Approach to Total Recovery
By Chris Prentiss

Addiction: A Disorder of Choice
By Gene M. Heyman

Truth about Addiction and Recovery
By Stanton Peele

Alcoholism: The Cause & the Cure
By Genita Petralli

Alternatives to Abstinence: A New Look at Alcoholism and the Choices in Treatment
By Heather Ogilvie

7 Tools to Beat Addiction
By Stanton Peele

Addiction Is a Choice
By Jeffrey A. Schaler, PhD

Resisting 12-Step Coercion: How to Fight Forced Participation in AA, NA, or 12-Step
By Stanton Peele

Alcoholics Anonymous: Cult or Cure?
By Charles Bufe

Addiction, Change & Choice: The New View of Alcoholism
By Vince Fox

Many Roads, One Journey: Moving Beyond the 12 Steps
By Charlotte S. Kasl, PhD

How Alcoholics Anonymous Failed Me: My Personal Journey to Sobriety through Self-Empowerment
By Marianne Gilliam

Coming Clean: Overcoming Addiction without Treatment
By Robert Granfield and William Cloud

Rational Recovery: The New Cure for Substance Addiction
By Jack Trimpey

Powerfully Recovered! A Confirmed 12 Stepper Challenges the Movement
By Anne Wayman

SOS Sobriety: The Proven Alternative to 12-Step Programs
By James Christopher

Sober for Good: New Solutions for Drinking Problems–Advice from Those Who Have Succeeded
By Anne M. Fletcher, MS, RD

Sex, Drugs, Gambling & Chocolate: A Workbook for Overcoming Addictions
By Dr. A. Thomas Horvath

Staying Clean & Sober: Complementary and Natural Strategies for Healing the Addicted Brain
By Merlene Miller, MA, and David Miller, PhD

When AA Doesn't Work for You: Rational Steps to Quitting Alcohol
By Albert Ellis, PhD, and Emmett Velten, PhD

Heavy Drinking: The Myth of Alcoholism as a Disease
By Herbert W. Fingarette

The Brain That Changes Itself: Stories of Personal Triumph from the Frontiers of Brain Science
By Norman Doidge, MD

As I finished this list of truth seekers, new solution leaders and associates I am fortified in my research and findings. I feel much the same as I did when I invented and created my combat fighting systems for the military and law enforcement communities. You now have a boatload of new resources from people that are much more educated in the fields of medicine, mind therapies and recovery than I am but yet are all saying the same thing. These came for me by just being observant, no different from the skills that you and others have.

In the next chapter I'm going to outline for you exactly what I did to get and stay clean and sober, reinvent my life and put myself on the steady fast track to success.

CHAPTER TWELVE

The Plan: Getting back on track and beyond to an outstanding life (Exactly what I did to eliminate alcohol and drugs from my life for good)

....

Here we are! This is what it all came down to for me—action—the action I was willing to take on a consistent basis until it became habit and part of my life where peace is now a central theme and positive forward-moving results are commonplace. This is a place where, yes I still think about escaping at times but now I just take action on about 30 different options as opposed to my old escape. In fact the idea of drinking or drugging is so removed from my thoughts and desires I sometimes wonder how that was part of my life at all.

Personal Recovery Program (PRP)

Your PRP is the 4th key and the method(s) you choose to use to create your addiction/excuse free life.

- Will it be meditation, therapy and Cognitive Behavior Training?
- Will it be a fitness plan, a diet plan, SMART recovery meetings and counseling with the wife?
- Will it be a two-week retreat where you do a personal time study, create a belief system log putting in place an "art of replacement" and "act as if" component coupled with Brain State Technologies training?
- Will it be Performance Mind Programming, a modified work schedule, a supplement schedule along with fitness, one-on-one and couples counseling?

You have to make a solid decision on what you're going to use. We heard it a thousand times but it's true, "If you fail to plan you're planning to fail."

NAME IT!

One of the first things that I decided to do was put a label on my new path, my recovery program, my set of actions. I felt if I put a name to my plan it would have more power. For me putting a name on this made it even more real.

Words have so much power for us. Allow me to demonstrate the power of one word. I have a *guest* friend coming over tonight so I won't be available or I have a *pest* of a friend coming over tonight so come bail me out. Small word change—"guest" or "pest"—but it has a huge meaning difference.

I called my journey my **OTBP—On Track and Beyond Path**. If you like you may want to call your path the **PRP (Personal Recovery Program)** or the **PDP (Personal Development Path).** My suggestion is to name it something that represents importance for you. It will take on an important role in your mind's eye and that's exactly where it needs to be. There's power in things that are important to us.

BREAK IT DOWN!

I got myself a notebook to write in and broke down my actions, putting them all on paper so they were organized and not floating around in my head. I chose to set things up in weeklong increments. What I mean by this is I would do several different activities daily for seven days at a time. Some activities would roll into the next week, some activities would be built upon, other activities would be replaced by new actions altogether. As we move forward you'll see how this will continue to play itself out, taking on different forms, and how I used this knowledge to get past the self-destructive and abusive lifestyle.

REVISIT PAST ACTION!

One of the keys to my OTBP was to look back at my history of actions. The following bullets were mentioned in the beginning of the book as things I wanted; behaviors that I displayed or a mind-set that I had that was a driving force for my stressed state and the feeling of discomfort ultimately resulting in the drink or drug. These are some of my old patterns of action...

- Be liked, fit in and stand out as a doer and leader and get that respect.
- I was a master artist at escaping from reality.
- I didn't feel accepted and unfortunately I wasn't, so most aspects

of my childhood were a fight to feel that I belonged.

- Often finding myself in antagonistic situations plus feeling uncomfortable unless I was excelling in all activities that I did.
- "Have attitude will travel" and "play harder, be better and you'll win them over."
- Birds of a feather flock together.
- You can't fly with the eagles if you hang with the turkeys.
- Hanging out with all the wrong people, going to all the wrong places, doing all the wrong things.

The above mentioned items were generally the central theme behind my discomfort which led to the desire to escape which resulted in drinking or drugging. Once I got to the core issues and changed the lens that I looked at my life through things were significantly easier. Let's take a look at each issue one by one.

- Be liked, fit in and stand out as a doer and leader and get that respect.

Once I framed this differently, my perspective and view changed immediately. I realized that the ones that mattered most in my life did respect me, they more than liked me they LOVED me. As a dad to five kids I finally truly saw the way they looked up to me and that to them I was their hero. This realization made me cry. All this time I was focusing on impressing the wrong people!

This was also true for my work, my staff and customers who really show me respect as a doer and a leader. I allow myself to honestly feel that now and I honestly give it back.

This first one was a biggie, as being liked and standing out as leader mattered greatly to me because of my environment growing up. I really took my time and truly looked at the relationships in my life, realizing I am enough just the way I am.

Let's take a look at another one: Often finding myself in antagonistic situations...

These were the situations that would sooner or later drive me to desire some type of pressure release. The first thing I had to recognize was that I was responsible for every situation that I was in. I may not have caused it but I was responsible for handling my part in it.

Upon greater evaluation I realized just from looking at this part of my life that obviously my crowd of friends was a big part of my problem. The reason I say greater evaluation is that even well into my adult years, I mean it wasn't like I was hanging out at strip clubs. It could have been the guys at the gym that liked to trash-talk or the gossip I kept allowing myself to be cornered by at my coffee shop or the old-time "friends" that would call and only want to talk about how bad life was for them. You get my drift? These were people who were always complaining and whining about this or that.

As you can see once you get into the rhythm things start really coming together and you can group or batch some of your own setups for feeling a certain way which drives your need to escape or to drink or drug!

This brings us to the following three that dove tail off antagonistic situations and the people I was spending time with.

- Birds of a feather flock together.
- You can't fly with the eagles if you hang with the turkeys.
- Hanging out with all the wrong people, going to all the wrong places, doing all the wrong things.

This one is pretty simple. I've heard that generally speaking we are an average of our five closest friends. Having said that if I'm serious about changing my life for the better just changing the groups that I spend time with has a major effect on the outcome of my life. Knowing that I can't fly with the eagles if I hang with the turkeys is absolutely key! You need to step up and find people who will inspire growth and change, not keep you in the same place. It made a phenomenal difference in my life when I finally did this.

- I was a master artist at escaping from reality.

As I mentioned before you and I are responsible for our lives, we can escape from reality for only a short time. Wherever we go there we are so we better learn to deal with our reality. If we're going to play this game of life you can make it much more enjoyable by learning to use healthy escapes as an avenue to help you shut the world out for a few minutes, hours or even days if needed.

Here's a list of some of my own personal healthy escapes I take when I feel I need a break.

Go for a mountain bike ride
Walk or run on the beach
Go to the gym and blast my music with the headphones on
Rent a movie and blast the volume
Fly my plane
Take my wife out to dinner
Take my daughters to the playground
Turning the ringer off of my phone for a day with appropriate
    message
Go to a bed and breakfast with my wife
Do fun activities with my boys
Bring something yummy home for dinner as a surprise for the family
Wax my car
Take a dip in the Jacuzzi
Walk around the lake with my wife
Do a kickboxing class
Ride my motorcycle
Draw with my daughters

Simply relax on a park bench or sit in my car without an agenda
Listen to my favorite motivational speakers on CD
Go for a drive with my wife and explore new neighborhoods

These are just some of the activities that I choose from to enjoy
when I need a break. What's more revealing is that all of these activities
are constructive and positive activities/habits. Once I recognized these as
the practices of a doer and a person that is living life to the fullest I felt
proud of myself for truly playing this game of life. Sure I have down moments or bad times just like anybody else. Only now I choose a construc-
tive/positive way to deal with them on a consistent basis, and the more
you do this the easier it will become.

- I didn't feel accepted and unfortunately I wasn't, so most aspects
  of my childhood were a fight to feel that I belonged.
- "Have attitude will travel" and "play harder, be better and you'll
  win them over."

I now know that not being accepted because of the color of my skin
is no excuse for my making bad decisions and anyone who subscribes to
that belief is someone I don't need as a friend or even bother with anyway.

Bottom line on acceptance, if I maintain being the man of God that
I should be for myself, my family and the universe around me and someone still doesn't like me it's probably not meant to be and I will not lose
sleep over it—I move on.

I travel everywhere I go with a positive attitude, live life to the best
of my abilities and I broadcast to the world my best efforts. That's all anybody can ask for.

For my PRP this covered about 75% of my themes and attitudes
around drinking and drugging. This gave me a massive immediate edge
over a habit that caused so many issues in my life.

The other two areas that I need to address are stressful issues and location/people triggers. Honestly after focusing on the top 75% of my themes and attitudes stressful issues became massively easier to handle with the healthy activities that I used for escaping. I guess being a person who is always looking for ways to better myself also helps. This comes in the form of taking classes, reading books, doing workshops in personal development, raising your kids, marriage, health and fitness, finances, work relationships, coping with butt-head neighbors, even selecting and dealing with your crooked auto mechanic.

Triggers really were straightforward for me. I wrote them down—certain people, a particular song, even a brand of European cigars—and came up with a plan on how I would deal with them if they came my way (which they always do).

Other triggers were locations, meaning certain bar areas, shady parts of town, some events where drinks were served, certain television shows, being away on long business trips or certain emotions that might come from being HALTE, that is, hungry, angry, lonely, tired and emotional (too high or too low).

After about 8 to 12 weeks I was about 80% good to go, the remaining 20% was the ability to manage my life stressors. This really meant making a better version of Hank, a better life for me and my family, personally and professionally.

Honestly I would say my past programming from the mainstream treatment culture is to blame for most of my mind screw. This whole idea that you're defective, morally bankrupt, powerless, that any good that you do comes from God alone and keeping it a requirement that you go to meetings to stay sober has great power to really screw with your mind. Especially if you were a part if it for more than a decade as I was.

"During my life I have to live it,
and at the end of my life,
I have to live with the life I had."

As time went on I developed a lot of new excellent habits and skills in dealing with people, events and financial occurrences that didn't happen to go my way and I will continue to learn as life marches on. Let's remember all skills are learnable!

Now that we've addressed my modus operandi, general themes and stressors behind my addictions, we can move onto what I did as far as daily new habits to set myself on a better path, the path of a "recovered alcoholic" or a "new man." I like to call it just a much better version of me.

Earlier in the book we talked about neuroplasticity and the idea of "neurons that fire together wire together." This refers to rewiring of the brain's circuitry and over time neurons (which can be a mind-set, a behavior or belief system) will be the new default setting taking over the old habit or behavior. Hence a new hardwired neuropathway, this is what "neurons that fire together wire together" implies. This also means that neurons that don't fire together—that atrophy, in other words—they no long have dominance over the brain's patterns of thought. It's like eating better foods. In the beginning your body and brain still want the french fries and you really have to work at not eating them but after three or four weeks of refraining your body wants those salads you've been eating and your brain is no longer fixated on the fries.

This is exactly how the brain works as long as you don't keep digging things up from the past, deepening your attachment to those things on a daily basis, like they do in the rooms. You will eventually totally forget about these things unless somebody else brings them to your attention.

This is the goal and result you're looking for in creating a new set of thinking and behavior patterns resulting in a totally new you. This is very similar to cognitive behavioral therapy.

What you see below is my personal recovery program which is really my lifestyle because what you see in week 11 through 12 is pretty much what I do every day. It is a significantly better and a much more well-rounded use of my time than going to AA meetings and listening to other people who have no focus on where they're going in life whine about their problems.

I will add that I used this as a basic guide to follow and to remember not to have a cow if you miss something. Additionally during weeks one through eight I took my life a little "lighter" than usual with extra focus on keeping those stressing people and places to an absolute minimum. This is exactly what you can do; just plug your best recovery methods in from chapter 10 and make it your very own personal program.

Okay, let's take a look...

Weeks 1-2	Weeks 3-4
8 glasses of water daily	8 glasses of water daily
Complete and balanced breakfast	Complete and balanced breakfast
Recovery supplements	Recovery supplements
Walking cardio, mind-setting 20 mins	Walk/run cardioX3/strengthX2, mind-setting 1 hr
Day planning 10 mins	Day planning 10 mins
Meditation 5 mins	Meditation 10 mins
Complete and balanced lunch	Complete and balanced lunch
Recovery reading daily 15 mins	Spiritual or soul-feeding reading 15 mins
Grateful list building session daily 5 - 10 mins	Self-esteem building session daily 5 - 10 mins
Trigger identification and replacement behavior planning plus handling problem. Done once at beginning and then based on day's activities you plan corrective actions.	Implementation of new actions with evaluation of new behaviors and adjustment at week's end.
Rest and relaxation daily	Rest and relaxation daily
Self-talk affirmations and incantations 5 - 7 mins	Self-talk affirmations and incantations 5 - 7 mins
Journaling daily 10 - 15 mins	Journaling daily 10 - 15 mins
Spiritual or soul-feeding reading 15 mins	Reading 15 mins
Complete and balanced dinner	Complete and balanced dinner
8 hrs sleep	8 hrs sleep

Week 5	Week 6
8 glasses of water daily	8 glasses of water daily
Complete and balanced breakfast	Complete and balanced breakfast
Recovery supplements	Recovery supplements
CardioX3/strengthX2, mind-setting 1 hr	CardioX3/strengthX3, mind-setting 1 hr
Day planning 10 mins	Day planning 10 mins
Meditation 10 mins	Meditation 15 mins
Complete and balanced lunch	Complete and balanced lunch
Recovery reading / spiritual or soul-feeding reading 15 mins	Personal growth / spiritual reading 15 mins
Self-concept building session daily 5 -10 mins	Building & listening to audio MP3 of gratefuls, self-esteem and new self-concept with affirmations while working out 30 mins
Implementation of new actions with evaluation of new behaviors and adjustment at week's end.	Implementation of new actions with evaluation of new behaviors and adjustment at week's end.
Rest and relaxation	Rest and relaxation
Self-talk affirmations and incantations 5 - 7 mins	Self-talk affirmations and incantations 5 - 7 mins
Journaling daily 10 - 15 mins	Journaling daily 10 - 15 mins
Reading 15 mins	Reading 15 mins
Complete and balanced dinner	Complete and balanced dinner
8 hrs sleep	8 hrs sleep

Weeks 7-8	Weeks 9-10
8 glasses of water daily	8 glasses of water daily
Complete and balanced breakfast	Complete and balanced breakfast
Recovery supplements	Recovery supplements
CardioX3/StrengthX3, mind-setting 1 hr	CardioX3/StrengthX3, mind-setting 1 hr
Day planning 10 mins	Day planning 10 mins
Meditation 15 mins	Meditation 15 mins
Complete and balanced lunch	Complete and balanced lunch
Reading 15 mins	Reading 15 mins
Listen to audio MP3 of grateful list, self-esteem and new self-concept with affirmations while working out 30 mins	Listen to audio MP3 of grateful list, self-esteem and new self-concept with affirmations while working out 30 mins
Be the new you with trigger handled and replacement behavior in place.	Be new Hank
Rest and relaxation	Rest and relaxation
Self-talk affirmations and incantations 5 - 7 mins	Self-talk affirmations and incantations 5 - 7 mins
Journaling daily 10 - 15 mins	Journaling daily 10 - 15 mins
Reading 15 mins	Reading 15 mins
Complete and balanced dinner	Complete and balanced dinner
8 hrs sleep	8 hrs sleep

Weeks 11-12

8 glasses of water daily
Complete and balanced breakfast
Recovery supplements
CardioX3/strengthX3, mind-setting 1 hr
Day planning 10 mins
Meditation 15 mins
Complete and balanced lunch
Reading 15 mins
Listen to MP3 of grateful list, self-esteem & new concept builders with goal visions during workout sessions. 30 mins
Be new Hank
Rest and relaxation
Self-talk affirmations and incantations 5 - 7 mins
Journaling daily 10 - 15 mins
Reading 15 mins
Complete and balanced dinner
8 hrs sleep

Daily checklist

Daily activity	Day	1	2	3
8 glasses of water				
Complete and balanced breakfast				
Recovery supplements daily				
Walking W/O cardio, mind-setting				
Self-affirmations and incantations				
Day planning				
Meditation 5 mins				
Complete and balanced lunch				
Recovery reading daily				
Grateful list building session				
Trigger identification and replacement behavior planning plus handling problem				
Rest and relaxation				
Journaling daily				
Spiritual or soul-feeding reading				
Complete and balanced dinner				
8 hrs sleep				

Going back to self-talk from earlier, I want you to remember there are conversations when you talk to other people and when other people talk to you but those conversations we have with **ourselves** are the absolute most important and carry the most weight! You know that big or small voice in your head telling you the good stuff or telling you the bad stuff... you really control this voice. This is why self-affirmation is so important. Affirm and believe with conviction you can and will change that voice inside.

After doing this for 90 days when you know that you've set your focus from the beginning and you're going to make a major change in your life it really becomes profound. Man I tell you what after doing this I was really a new Hank. This is exactly the type of mental and action-oriented focus that we create in our training for military and law enforcement operators—of desired results going further, getting there faster and achieving it with less effort. No questions asked.

Creating my own program was right for me and works for thousands of other people. You may be a person who either (a) would like to have someone create it for you (if so that's excellent and use what works for you), or B) feels in the beginning you would like more help and you may not trust yourself just yet. That's totally cool too. Do what you think is going to work best for you, just please don't kid yourself. There can be a high price to pay if things don't go your way. If you get arrested your whole life could be changed forever. If you kill someone driving drunk not only your life but someone else's life and their family's life will be changed forever, how would that make you feel? I hope you get my point. I know friends, or better put I did know friends, that wanted that one last-time thing...and their life ticket was pulled.

Please take your choices for your recovery program seriously—it's your life.

Whether you make an OTBP for yourself or choose a lighter or even heavier recovery route there are a few areas that you'll want to make sure are covered in your focus. If you're going away to a program make sure most of these components listed are covered during your stay or are addressed for when you get home. If most of these aren't covered I would ask the intake consultant how you should handle them. That will tell you a lot about the program. These issues will not handle themselves.

Environment – If drinking is your thing and you live over a bar it's probably going to be hard to stay straight. Some people do achieve it but I wouldn't put my money on that bet. If you live in an environment where there's lots of stress, triggers and disharmony or you're extremely unhappy it's going to be harder to achieve abstinence from whatever it is that you use to cope. It has been said environment is the factor that people stress over more than any other. Maybe it's because your environment is constantly working against you. Do your best to make your environment work for you—not against you.

Your temple (your body) – You have only one, but seriously we talked about this earlier. You can do so much to get your body on track and feeling great within a few weeks no longer craving your nemesis. Once you get your body working for you again and not against you you'll wonder why this isn't in the mainstream for everybody. You'll want to make a list of your additional habits that aren't good for the body such as smoking, too much caffeine, unhealthy eating habits, not sleeping, etc. Again, the way you treat your body is going to be directly reflected in you, if you take care of your body, your body will take care of you. Remember you're not going to be able to do good unless you feel good.

Your support system – I can't say enough about the importance of having a support system. I'm not talking about an enabler but a support system/person or group of people that are really there for you in your decision to change your life's direction from your addiction. Having the support of one's mate or spouse or close loved one can make all the difference for the person breaking free from their nemesis. Knowing you're supported and loved through this process is priceless and adds such a dimension to your sobriety/clean life that will assist you in reaching even higher. Knowing I had my wife by my side to help me made me feel like it was totally possible and I was never alone—YES!

Methods for handling stress and problem-solving systems - Just because we've decided to stop and clean up our lives doesn't mean stress and life's challenges stop too. As a matter of fact experts say we generally have a sizable life challenge every 60 to 90 days. Like I said before, whether it's meditation, running, the boxing gym or cooking for others, having an outlet that you transition to for dealing with stress is essential.

Another common denominator in balanced living is having a method or process for dealing with life's problems and not letting our worries get the best of us. This can be as simple as writing the problem down on a sheet of paper, putting a line down the middle of the page on one side list all the things that could possibly happen if the problem were true and on the other side write down all the possible solutions. Circle the top three, then sleep on it. Ask yourself, a trusted friend or God for the best answer and when you wake up pick one and get to work on it. This is an exercise I do all the time.

Some people have a mastermind group of successful trusted people they run things by. The point and goal is to have a positive outlet for dealing with stress and solving life's problems.

Goals, dreams and visions – Your goals, dreams and mental visions have magnetic power. They pull you in their direction, they create drive in your heart and if you focus on them on a consistent basis they will fuel a fire in you so big you'll wonder how you ever had time for an addiction or would even waste your life on such emptiness. In case you didn't know I wanted to mention that 3% of the population control 97% of the world's wealth. That 3% know they have to be goal and purpose driven—they are leaders with a vengeance.

Education – Books, audio programs, live events and videos or DVDs - Investing in your education always pays off, however in this area I cannot say enough. Books, audio programs, live events and video have furthered my life more than any other medium. If I didn't mention earlier it was one book that started it and completely opened my eyes to the whole new world of recovery. From that day forward my life has been changed for the better. Each book you read and program/class you take arms you with more information, and the more information you have, the better choices you can make.

Your self-talk – We talked about this a bit earlier—what you say to yourself is huge. When you talk yourself into or out of drinking, drugging, gambling, spending or whatever, this is the little voice inside with big power. This voice has the power to get you to do or not do things. Watch out for that devil on your shoulder that moves you closer to trouble inch by inch. You have to know what he's up to so you can control him. Really think about what you're thinking about. Again there are boatloads of information out there on this topic. We include some earlier in this chapter and you can also find information about this on our website and at our live events.

We've covered a lot of things that I personally used to get my life back and take it to a new level. We discussed what the main components are of a solid program that will put you well on your way back to the life that you want and more.

This is all based on wanting much more than what the mainstream program can offer you. I've made an assumption that if you've stayed with me this far, you want an extraordinary life and you're willing to take charge of your life, take action, measure your results and then take more action until you get the life you want. I hope I am right.

If you didn't guess by now I really want to see the best in people. All of us have greatness inside but it's impossible to bring it out with the effects of an addiction beating us down, reeking havoc in all areas of our lives.

There's a story in the bible about how a group of people were camped right next door to the Promised Land. They were so excited and couldn't wait to share in all the greatness that the land had to offer, all they had to do was show they would put up a fight for what was already promised by God to be theirs. You would think heck they would at least have tried to fight for it, it had already been proven that God was a man of his word. You would think they would be filled with faith, charged and ready to kick ass.

Believe it or not they said, nope it's impossible, it's never gonna happen. Their negative attitude prevented them from even starting. So for the next 40 years they stayed right next door to exactly what they wanted, whining to one another and not taking action.

I tell this story to illustrate that this was me for over a decade. I knew there was something better out there but I wouldn't take action, because the masses were telling me different. My small voice inside said to me "You're just a powerless, sick, alcoholic and you always will be. You're defective so just do what you're told." For a long time I didn't bother to look outside the box.

Well today I'm the voice telling you to look outside the box, break the box, burn the box. I can bet your promised land is right next to you right now. I bet you know that and you've been able to wrap your hand around it but you blink and it's up the block again and you say how did it get way up there so fast?

I promise you if you take charge of your life and mix your ideas with inspiration you can make it happen. Don't ever let me hear you say ideas are nothing. Ideas are everything and they are tangible. Every building, every home was first a vision in someone's mind, then a rough sketch on paper, then an engineering plan, on to a master building plan, then the construction and finally the home or building that we are now in. It all started with an idea, a thought, a dream.

These ideas, dreams and visions must become so strong that you're so inspired to take action. That there is no other option than to bring it to life!

Believe that the life that you want is possible for you. If I can do it and hundreds of thousands of other people did it you can too! If you have fallen down, *so what?* Get back up! Anything worthwhile is not going to be easy. Champions are champions because they have comeback power. You must attain your comeback power and be a champion in your own life!

So get to work and make it real. This is the biggest part of the miracle process. It always blows me away when people want that life, want that job, bitch and moan about not being able to buy their kids this or that, are pissed that the neighbors are always going on vacation but are not willing to take that night class to learn the extra skills to move up in their work. I'm gonna tell you straightaway if you want to better your life, you're going to have to claim it, you're going to have to work for it! Yes there are a few people who have it on easy street, I suppose, but they are so few and far between and those who don't work for what they have generally don't value what they have anyway. If you value it you'll protect it, you'll fight to keep it.

Again we're talking about making your life monumentally better. If you want to just get off the addiction that's great, but I promise you after you do some of our life-expanding exercises in this book, on our website or from our live events, you will want more than just to get clean and sober. Know that you're going to have to appreciate and welcome discipline into your life to make it happen.

After doing all this great work you want to make sure your life is always going in the direction that you want it to and to also know when you're off track. You will ensure this by using the 5th and final key:

Lifetime Monitoring System (LMS)

The lifetime monitoring system is your daily head-to-toe check-up. It's just like the preflight check pilots do: You check all parts of the functioning system before you take flight. You even do mental and emotional check to see if you're good to go for flight. The way this plays out for me is when I'm feeling some kind of a way I ask myself what's going on and why might I be feeling this way? Am I just tired from a long day of work? Have I been sleeping in hotel after hotel during a business trip? Have I not worked out or am I stressed out from events in my life?

Often if I just sit down with no distractions for 10 to 15 minutes I can get a grip on what's going on and address the issues or topics that are troubling or concerning me. Sometimes I need to go to dinner with my wife and during that evening through conversation we together figure it out or sometimes I figure it out alone just by having my wife as a sounding board.

There are other times I just need some alone time, which may mean taking a walk, riding my motorcycle, taking the plane for a blast. Sometimes just watching my son play football or my five-year-old twin daughters play in the park is all it takes. Then there are other times it's deeper than that and I may need a vacation from life or I may even need to escalate my solutions to a greater level and talk to my pastor or a professional if that's what it takes and sometimes it is. Bottom line, we can get through anything with the right resources without falling back on bad habits or actions. And even if we do fall back on a bad habit or choose a bad action we can ALWAYS pick ourselves up and start over again. All champions have fallen down a time or 10; they're champions because they get back up.

Remember that you are a champion! Never believe anyone else's negative picture of you. You chart your course, you set your sail, you sail your ship—you take responsibility for your results!

Make your life the way you want it!

I'd love to close out this reading with some fluffy, "go get 'em tiger" line, but it would be just that, a line. You are going to hit roadblocks and yours are going be different than mine or the guy's or girl's next to you. We are all unique with unique challenges. But so what? Walk through it, go over it, dig under it, ask for help, but if you want the life and I know that you do, do what it takes to claim yours.

And lastly don't B.S. yourself. You might be one of those guys that puts this book down and quits your addictions, goes on to make your life exactly the way you want it and the rest is history. However if you're like most of us you're going to have to make a huge commitment to making a better life, create a picture, build a plan, ask for help, get to work, fall down, get back up, bleed a little, cry a little, smile a lot, and get to the finish line with others around you.

In order to do this as we discussed over and over it's best if you have a plan to follow. These are our five keys to an addiction-free life.

1) **TPK – True perspective knowledge:**
   Your new fresh perspective based on true research date.

2) **PBL – Power Baseline:**
   Knowing what others have successfully done to get exactly what you want.

3) **PTP – Personal Trigger Points:**
   All the big and little things that personally set you off.

4) **PRP – Personal Recovery Program:**
   The methods you choose to use to create your addiction free life.

5) **LMS - Lifetime Monitoring System:**
   Daily head to toe check up to keep you running smoothly.

In closing on this book I want you to know that it is my wish for you that, whatever is holding you back, you make the time to push past it, find what you need inside of yourself and declare that it's your time now.

My mentors constantly say to me never lose sight of a goal, a dream or a planning session without setting the next step to achieve it. So right now, I mean right NOW, stop and set up what your next step will be. Figure out your first step to get right or to help that person in your life. Whether it be cutting up your credit card, emptying the pantry, calling your dealer and dropping a hammer, whether it be giving this book to that someone at the right time, talking to your brother's wife about his drinking, whatever it is plan it now and then take action today.

I'll say to you what my father-in-law, who is my second hero after my Dad, said to me. This is a man who has a loving wife, seven kids, 15 grandkids and 47 patented inventions and is a recent American Motorcycle Association hall of famer. "You can do whatever you set your mind to, nothing is impossible and don't ever let anyone tell you different, Hank. Now get out there, run your race and win."

I, Hank Hayes, support you 100%! IF you want it, you can do it! Okay, I'll say it... Go get 'em tiger!

> *"As a man thinketh in his heart, so he is."*
> − Proverbs 23:7˜

TRUE ADDICTION-FREE SHORT STORIES:

A collection of 9 true short stories from others who got back on track without the mainstream industry

. . . .

In the following pages of this book there are several "how I did it my way," sober short stories. They greatly vary in content, there is one from a gal who talks about needing alcohol the way humans need oxygen and then overcoming that to become a major inspirational woman in the business world, as a matter of fact she now runs a company called Become a 6-Figure Woman. You'll read another story from a gal who was an incest victim and binge drinker who found the freedom to cope with life without alcohol, so much so that it never even occurs to her now to reach for a drink ever. You'll read a story called "Jew in Jail," written by a guy who was sentenced to seven years in prison and fought to get his life back. The reason these stories are here in this book is for you to find something in them that you can relate to and see for yourself that there are as many ways to clean up your life as there are different types of people in the world.

DEEP HEALING

By Michelle Kulp

Alcohol was my lifeline. I needed it. Not the way you "need" a new pair of shoes or a new coat, but the way you need oxygen... to breathe...to stay alive. I picked up a bottle of Jack at age 13 and over the next 16 years we became best friends.

Alcohol was my escape from a painful reality that I couldn't seem to make sense of. It was a remedy to all my problems. At least it seemed that way at the time. You see, alcohol magically gave me a voice; it calmed my anxiety and was truly a social elixir for my deep-seated shyness and inhibitions. Essentially alcohol gave me a much needed boost for my low self-image.

Alcohol never made me unhappy; it was more that I drank because I was unhappy. Underneath the confident façade that the alcohol created was a frightened, insecure, terrified child.

I couldn't function without the alcohol. I didn't ease into drinking Jack Daniels either. I started out at the gate at age 13 drinking a pint of Jack straight up by myself. That's what my mind and spirit needed to ease the pain in my heart and soul. I felt a deep level of rejection in my life and alcohol helped me cope.

When I was drunk I felt powerful and in control...like I was on top of the world; but when the alcohol wore off, those feelings disappeared. As time went on, I needed more and more alcohol to cope. I never had the trigger in my brain that told me when to stop either. It was never enough.

Passing out was usually the way I stopped drinking for the night. Blackouts were the norm. So were 2-day hangovers, heart palpitations, anxiety, having no memory of driving home, being late for work, abusive relationships...the list goes on.

Looking back now, it felt like I was trying to "erase" me.

I didn't want to be here. I wanted to be somewhere else or be someone else; someone who was worthy. Growing up I always daydreamed of being someone else—television stars like Barbara Eden from *I Dream of Jeannie* or Samantha from *Bewitched*, or I'd take any of the angels from *Charlie's Angels*. I wanted to be anybody but me.

And so my life spiraled out of control for 16 years. Some good decisions intertwined with a lot of poor decisions made from my alcohol-infused brain. The consequences of the poor decisions gnawed away even more of my already low self-esteem. At age 21, I gave birth to my beautiful son. At age 23, I gave birth to my beautiful daughter, and then again at age 25, I gave birth to my second beautiful daughter.

When you're single and your life is out of control that's one thing, but when you become a parent and are entrusted with three magnificent beings who need and depend on you, it changes everything. At least it did for me.

Those three children saved my life because they gave me a reason to live.

I believe now that God blessed me with three children because that's what it took to settle my rebellious and reckless behavior.

When my children were ages 3, 5 and 8, I finally put the bottle down. After a heavy night of drinking Jack Daniels, not remembering how I drove home or anything from the previous evening, I woke up in psychic, emotional and physical pain. I sat in the bathroom, sick to my stomach, and had an epiphany: If I continued drinking like I was, I would be dead in a year. I wanted to live more than I wanted to die, so I stopped drinking that day in 1993 and have not drank alcohol since.

From that day forward, I began to nurture, feed and breathe life into that forgotten part of myself—the perfect, worthy self.

After I stopped drinking the emotional pain was almost more than I could bear. Not only did I have to deal with and heal my past, the one I was trying to erase and recover from, but I had 16 years of poor behavior and decision-making that brought on tremendous guilt, shame and self-loathing.

Drinking helped me cope. Not drinking made me feel vulnerable and exposed to the world. I was "naked" with no coping mechanisms.

That was the beginning of my healing, a long, long journey of healing, forgiveness, transformation, and self-love. A journey back to my true self.

When you drink excessively you drown your emotions; when you get sober, you learn to go through the emotions you used to avoid, to bring them out of the darkness and into the light where they can be healed. It's not an easy path.

The process that took me from that painfully low place to where I am today involved God, love, patience and faith. And the tools I used were therapy with a licensed clinical social worker to move through the pain; self-help books to give me new ways of coping and healing; seminars to learn from others who were ahead of me; a church where I was surrounded by supportive like-minded people, meditation to calm my over-analytical and fear-filled mind, exercise to give me the endorphins my body craved, healthy food for my neglected body, and good relationships with family and friends.

Instead of filling the void with alcohol, I filled it with God. I reconnected with the infinite love and forgiveness that God is; it filled me up. I learned to trust, to have faith and to know that God was making "straight" my crooked path.

I took one step, then another, then another—church, books, seminars, exercise, nutrition, etc. I just kept making more healthy choices and building on each one. I found support through my therapist, my life coach, healthy friends, Unity Church, and an inordinate amount of books. Books were everything to me. They transformed my unhealthy thinking to healthy thinking.

By grace, I was transformed. By faith, I was made whole. The old me had to die for the new me to be born. It was a long, arduous, painful journey, but the lessons were meaningful and deep. My prayer is still always that I continue to be healed deeply.

When you give yourself the "gifts" of meditation, contemplation and prayer, you find God within. You hear that still small voice that guides you, loves you unconditionally and wants you to be happy, joyous and free so that you may lead the path for others, holding the light in front of them, as others have done for me.

We are all connected to one another and intrinsically we are all equal. No one is more special than another. I feel very blessed with my life as it is now. I took a leap of faith in 2000 to leave an unhappy career in the legal field and follow my dreams of writing, teaching, speaking and coaching. I run an online business (www.becomea6figurewoman.com) and I connect with so many wonderful women around the globe. My mission is to inspire, educate and motivate women to believe in themselves and to find their true purpose in life. I believe most of us realize only a fraction of the potential we have inside and I give women permission to play BIG and to tap into that dormant potential that exists in each one of us.

My three wonderful children each had their own struggles with alcohol and drugs for a decade of my life. I was relentless and would not give up on those kids. I would not lose the fight to the drugs and alcohol; my kids deserved to live and be happy. They each came to sobriety in their own unique way and I am very proud of them.

My youngest daughter has over three years of sobriety, my other daughter has two years and my son has almost three years. My two daughters are in the program, but my son and I both came to our sobriety without the program.

We all are unique individuals yet we all have the same needs and goals: to live a happy, joyous, peaceful, prosperous, fun life! Whatever path takes you to that place is your special path.

Just know that underneath everything is the perfection that is you!

JEW IN JAIL

By Gary Goldstein

As soon as I was arrested on June 13, 1998, and then ultimately sentenced to seven years in prison (I actually served just under six), I knew that I had to finally get clean in order to live my life the way that it was always intended to be lived.

So, not long after I was sent upstate to one of the many prisons that comprise the New York State Department of Correctional Services, I began writing my book, *Jew in Jail*, which not only chronicled my day-to-day journey behind bars but also served as the stepping stone to finally deciding to get clean.

I had been actively drinking and drugging as well as gambling for well over 20 years at that point, and although I was now separated from the general public as a prisoner with a number, there were many opportunities to "score" drugs while incarcerated.

However, I chose to abstain and make this the turning point in my life.

I attended hundreds, if not thousands, of AA, NA and GA meetings behind bars, and although I didn't always like what I saw or experienced around me, I adhered to the concepts and kept in mind that selfishness in this case was a virtue.

Specifically, I didn't much care to see many members of these groups. Their very first act upon entering the meeting room would be to run to grab a cup of coffee off the table. I felt that they were simply replacing one addiction with another and I realized that it was the behavior, as much as the drug itself, that made one an addict.

So simply by observing others around me, I learned what I didn't want to turn into, if I hadn't already reached that same point in my disease as well.

After being released from prison on June 8, 2004, I immediately went to work in the construction industry. At the time, I had been clean for over six years. I also attempted to have my book published, although with minimal success.

My parole officer then ordered me to attend an outpatient drug program, which I completed in six short months.

It wasn't long after that I, feeling overconfident, succumbed to my urges and relapsed.

That without a doubt, as I now know today, was my rock bottom and I knew that I had no other choice but to get help if I didn't want a repeat of the past.

So I voluntarily entered into an outpatient program at Coney Island Hospital in Brooklyn, New York, and attended a full day's worth of meetings every day from Monday through Friday to unload the heavy burden I had been carrying deep inside all my life.

It was only then that I finally understood that the nature of my addiction was based on a lack of self-esteem, low self-confidence and feelings of underachievement.

Fortunately, though, I had my book to turn back to which was something that I spent five years on and revealed all of my innermost thoughts in when writing.

By scaling my book down several hundred pages and getting it republished it brought me back to my time incarcerated and to all of my thoughts on what I needed to do upon my release from prison.

After graduating from that outpatient drug program at Coney Island Hospital, I began a health regimen whereby I ate only low-fat foods, drank enormous amounts of water, took vitamins and worked out five days a week to get my body in shape to go along with my mind, which I continue to do today.

As an alumni member of that program, I speak to other clients trying to get themselves clean and sober, as well as visit patients in the detox unit and speak to any other groups that we travel to see.

Throughout this whole time in my life—beginning with my arrest and continuing to today—my family has been extremely supportive of me and I know that without them in my corner, my journey would be that much more difficult.

Sadly, my father and hero, Irving Goldstein, passed away from the effects of lung cancer and emphysema on January 23, 1999, while I was still on Rikers Island waiting to be sent upstate to serve my time.

I know that my father would have been very proud of my attempts to get clean and sober, although I also know myself that the journey never ends and I have to live with this disease one day at a time.

In closing, I can say without a doubt that my life today is much better being clean and sober, as I now have three and a half years of sobriety under my belt, and I implore anyone who has found any similarities to my story to go get the help he or she needs.

Simply put, it is NEVER too late and each and every one of us, who are all unique in our own way, deserve the best possible life we can make for ourselves.

The time is NOW!

THE STORY OF JULIE DVOSKIN

My name is Julie Dvoskin and I would like to share my story of a journey through addiction to the triumph of freedom. Growing up I was a normal child with a wonderful family. Somewhere in the transition between child- and adulthood, going through the growing pains of puberty, I lost myself in the process of trying to find myself. I was always a quiet teenager and good student but as I entered high school, I started hanging with the wrong crowd.

As the result of trying to fit in with the "cool kids" I started to experiment with marijuana, drinking and recreational drugs. I kept up appearances at home in front of my family until what I now realize was the turning point of my life.

Shortly after graduation I moved out on my own, went to college and worked, although my busy schedule did not stop me from partying with my friends.

One day, when I was on my way to work a truck struck me. That was the beginning of the end for me. Due to the accident, I sustained an injury to my back, which consisted of two herniated disks in my spine. I was sent to a back specialist and physical therapy where I was introduced to strong painkiller medication called Percocet. That became the love of my life, which eventually spiraled completely out of control.

Before I knew it, I was so addicted that I was ready to give up my dignity, my family that was so dear to me, my boyfriend and my life. This whirlwind lasted for 10 years! I started with painkillers and ended with living on the floors of strange people's houses, snorting cocaine, heroin and crystal meth and taking any drugs that came in my path.

When I could no longer hide my addiction from my family, the inevitable happened. They were in a complete state of shock. My family knew something was wrong but because they never saw what an addiction looks like, they were not aware of the signs, especially since I hid them so well! My mother, with whom I am extremely close, was so heartbroken. She tried every possible way to help me, from psychiatrists and the best specialists to fortune-tellers and eventually every sort of medication.

All mainstream treatment attempts were in vain. This process lasted a few years and I truly believed that my destiny was to die as an addict. I found myself hopeless and waiting to die! I started praying to God to help me, even though I knew nothing about him and was far from the topic of religion. Shortly after that, my mom responded to an advertisement in the newspaper about a rehabilitation center and was invited to a church.

There we found out that an addiction is not a physical problem but rather a spiritual one. And that's why all the methods we tried were ineffective. We were approaching the issue from the wrong angle. Thank God for that!

I went to the Love Rehabilitation Center in Germany and enrolled in the Way to Freedom program. It has been a year since I came back from Germany. I am now living an exquisite, brand-new life with God. I am free of all addiction and I am finally happy. I am studying to be a psychiatrist and would like to implement spirituality into the world of psychiatry. I would like to bring reform into this world and change the view of addiction in this society. Currently I am fully dedicated in helping at the Love Rehabilitation Center of the Embassy of God church in Philadelphia. I am also involved in working with the youth and my church. I want to speak at schools and major events to reach as many young people as possible and tell them my story. I want to work with girls and help them achieve self-confidence and avoid sexual mistakes. I am completely committed to serving God and helping others.

THE MARILYN BRADFORD STORY

Hi my name is Marilyn Bradford and I would like to invite you to a different possibility dealing with addiction.

I have struggled with my own addictions since childhood, when I was so addicted to sugar that my parents had to limit how much money per day I could spend on candy! Later I developed addictions to cigarettes, food and alcohol, not to mention my addictions to being a victim and to trying to "get it right." (Addiction can take many forms, but it is always the same energy. That is why people who seem to have cleared one addiction will become addicted to something else. They are just changing their target.)

What I didn't understand at the time was that I was actually choosing the state of being addicted as a way to cope with other choices and misinterpretations of life and it's events that I had made.

Now I no longer have to obsess about alcohol or any addiction, nor do I have to follow anyone else's prescribed program of behavior. For the first time in my life, I have true choice.

My own recovery was a long and difficult process filled with much trauma and drama. Too bad I didn't know then what I know now!

After teaching high school for five years and earning a Master's in Education, I went on to work in a number of different fields, drinking and smoking and over- or under eating through it all. Finally, over 20 years ago, with a marriage failing and drinking myself into oblivion almost every night, I entered psychotherapy. I was fortunate to find a talented nontraditional therapist who helped me to begin to unravel the web of lies and crazy belief systems I had bought from others and created for myself. After working together for awhile, he sent me to a 12-step program to solidify my recovery, as that seemed the best available option at the time. By that point my marriage had fallen apart, I was dealing with depression and I was alienated from my family. However, I had managed to not drink for months and was beginning to have a glimpse of a life without alcohol. Shortly thereafter I entered a graduate program to become a therapist with a specialty in addiction. Upon graduating, I worked for three and a half years in a psychiatric hospital, where I ran the adult trauma unit. I then went into private practice. Over the next few years I grappled with the paradox working to stay sober by admitting my powerlessness and turning my life and will over to someone or something greater than me, while at the same time taking classes on the importance of empowering individuals. I also learned about other programs for recovery and I tried them all. Somehow applying someone else's answer to my addiction seemed to require an enormous amount of effort for a pretty unsatisfactory result. Yes, I remained sober, but at a great cost to my being. I was told I had to have an identity as an alcoholic and that I had to put in hours of work to stay sober. The difficulty for me was that I actually desired to have a life, and I desired to be able to offer my clients more than what seemed to be available.

What a relief it was to me to find Access Consciousness. Finally there were tools and techniques and processes that I could learn and apply to my life and remaining issues with addiction. I began teaching the tools to my clients with amazing results! There was no longer a need to approach addiction using someone else's way. Possibilities and choices became available to people that they had not known existed. Ultimately, each person became responsible for picking up the tools and applying them to their life, or choosing not to. The results were so different from what I knew from psychotherapy or traditional treatment that I asked the founder of Access, Gary Douglas, if we could start a program for addiction based on Access. This was the beginning of Right Recovery for You, LLC.

If you are willing to have an open mind, to consider letting go of limiting belief systems and the way you have been told things are or even seem to be, if you are willing to begin to learn to trust you and your knowing, using these tools and techniques can change your life in ways you never thought possible. We do not offer a system that you fit yourself into. We do not tell you what to do or give you answers about your life. Only you know how all of your issues began. What we offer is designed to acknowledge what you know as the creator of your life and to help you get to the place where you can identify where this began so you can change it. We give you tools and techniques and the results are up to you. This is YOUR choice. It may seem a little scary, yet with courage and determination you can create the life that you truly desire.

Move a Mountain—
Bring a Shovel:
How I Overcame
Addiction without
AA or Twelve Steps

By Chad Miller

My name is Chad. I'm a recovered alcoholic. My drinking career began at the young age of 17 while I was a junior in high school. An honor student and military academy candidate, I showed tremendous promise for a bright and successful future. The world was my proverbial oyster. But I would ultimately trade the pearl for short-term euphoria. No one of us sets out on life's journey determined to become an addict. Addiction creeps in over time, wearing away the spirit and emotional strength of the user like a river wears down a river stone, tumbling and polishing the rock until it's no longer recognizable as it once existed in its original state. Once a boulder atop a lofty mountain overlooking my vast destiny landscape, I woke some 25 years later only to find myself a grain of sand on the desolate shore of addiction, tumbled and washed over time, dashed against rock after rock, hard place after hard place—the direct result of my turbulent struggle with alcohol.

After graduating college, I spent several years wandering aimlessly from one management job to the next—each one as unfulfilling as the

previous. Constantly battling to stay afloat in the raging waters of my addiction, holding down a stable job consumed my energy. When not working like a madman at my nine-to-five occupation (more like eight-to-seven
or two-to-midnight, depending on the job situation), I invested my time—
and money—in alcoholic pursuits.

Within a short period of time, I managed to accumulate multiple
DUI offenses and spent a total of several months in jail as a result. In addition to the mounting incarcerations, my exposure to court-ordered drug
and alcohol rehabilitation services escalated. At one point, I even entered
into an intensive, in-house drug and alcohol rehabilitation treatment
center completing a 37-day program. Although these latter experiences in
treatment were not without their merits, my struggle with alcohol eventually continued. I experienced long periods of sobriety followed by periods
of "testing the chemical waters," each time emerging more disappointed
and frustrated than the last time, compounding my feelings of self-pity
and hopelessness.

Until one day, while transcribing the journal I logged while involved
in the 37-day rehab program during the winter of 2000 to publish in my
memoir, I was reminded of the subtle but powerful anecdotes shared by
one of the counselors there. He said, "God can and will move that mountain for you, my friend. But you have to bring a shovel."

While I typed these words into the word processing application of my
laptop, it was as if the sun shone through the dark clouds of the terrible
storm raging all around me—this alcoholism. I had been sober for two
months, setting aside the magic elixir all on my own. I turned away from
the bottle cold turkey. I knew then I had resolved deep within my very
soul never to use drugs or alcohol again. I can honestly say, for the first
time since I'd started drinking more than 25 years ago, it was something
I never wanted to engage in again. Like one who has burned one's hand
over a flame and knows immediately to avoid such activity lest he suffer
the inevitable consequence of his action, I made the resolute and absolute decision to abstain from using drugs or alcohol the rest of my life. I

knew I had to share with others the fact that it can be done—that you can walk away from your addiction without the help of any 12-step program or magnanimous support vehicle. I knew this as sure as I knew my own name.

My name is Chad. I'm a recovered alcoholic. I control my own behavior. The substance does not control me. I make the conscious decision to drink or not drink—to use or not use. I have moved mountains in my past and will move them again. Somewhere along the way, I forgot to bring my shovel. But I once again possess my shovel—my strength. And these mountains will move.

You must find your personal shovel—that tool or mechanism which allows you to move forward. Motivation is different for each of us. Ask yourself: What is it that drives me to forge ahead? Somewhere deep within each of us is a unique character trait which has been assigned genetically; it's embedded in our DNA, by a universal force greater than ourselves. Find that tool—that shovel. Live each day as if it were your last. Do not squander your talents. You are significant. You are important. You are loved. You are needed—by someone. You were created for a specific reason, not by accident. Move that mountain one shovel load at a time. And it never hurts to ask others to help you by digging alongside you. Through helping others, you just may find the one you help the greatest is yourself.

MY STORY...

By Scott Rossel

L ike many young college men, I was aimless and bored. So naturally, it wasn't difficult finding distractions. I had no purpose. I had no idea what I truly enjoyed doing and I had no idea who I wanted to be. Religion never really worked for me and having an above-average IQ didn't help me make a lot of friends. But one friend, who loved to go to sporting events, captured my attention. He had season tickets to everything and I was always invited. We had great seats and there was always a pretty waitress there to bring us drinks that he was all too willing to pay for. One season turned into another, then another, and before I knew it, I had dropped out of college, got a nice-paying job and figured out how to drink on a daily basis while still making a fairly decent living. I became a functional drunk.

My job had only one redeeming value; an ample paycheck. But I hated the work and the people I worked with. It was only the bottle of bourbon I had ready access to that made the days bearable. At the time, I was also suffering from a health condition that to this day has never been properly diagnosed, much less cured. I would inexplicably fall asleep for four hours during the day. I was always cranky and my stomach was a mess. Oddly, the alcohol seemed to help. I lost that job...and several others.

An acquaintance of mine had been arrested for drunk driving and was forced to attend AA. He was constantly complaining about "the steps" and having to sit in a smelly room full of losers. I dismissed AA because it all sounded like a bunch of religious rattle trap on top of poor pseudoscience. My friend was in AA for three months before he had too much to drink and drove off a bridge to his death. I was not impressed. He had the Big Book. He had the 12 steps. He had a room full of like-minded and supportive individuals. He had a sponsor. And now he has a really nice plot in a well-wooded canyon his mother paid a considerable amount for with a beautiful black granite gravestone.

I knew I had a problem with alcohol. But I also knew I made the decision to drink and could just as easily make the decision not to. So I did. It didn't work. As soon as things got rough, I went back to the bottle.

Then I found the solution. It started with an old book I found that insisted that everyone should take the time to meditate and find the person they really are inside—to find purpose in life. This sounded great, but the book offered no method to do so. I made it my quest to find or create a method and after reading several self-help books that gave a few clues, it finally came to me one night—over a very expensive bottle of cask strength scotch: "Whatever puts a smile on your face is the closest you will ever get to your true purpose in life." I expanded on this idea and figured out how to brainstorm all of the things in life that gave me purpose, direction and passion.

I still had my health condition which constantly held me back, but I found purpose in a new direction and returned to college. I also started a hobby in electronics and computers. And I found challenge and passion in a new job. I also found my health condition an even bigger challenge. I decided I would solve my problem even if doctors couldn't figure it out. And I did—well, mostly. Of course, the alcohol was part of the problem in spite of feeling like the cure. I found my specific life purpose and greatest passions and focused my attentions on them whenever I felt like I needed a drink. And it worked. I also focused on researching my health problem and found a very useful solution. (That's a different story, but the punch line is chromium picolinate. It works...somewhat.)

One day, another acquaintance of mine, who faced challenges with alcohol and drugs, noticed a list I kept on my bathroom mirror along with some useful quotes. I kept them there as a constant reminder each day to maintain focus. He was most intrigued by the phrase "I am an Explorative Archivist." He had never heard of such a thing and was wondering why I would have it on my bathroom mirror. When I explained that it was my unique life purpose and that I rediscovered it using a method I had devised, he insisted I show him how. I did. Two months later, he had given up alcohol and drugs, reconciled his relationship with his parents, graduated college, moved to France and started a restaurant with a distant relative. He had found his purpose in life and never looked back at alcohol to solve his problems.

This same success path—the mere methods I used to find purpose and passion in life just to get through the day—ended up being a central theme in the success of several of my friends and their acquaintances. More than once I was told I should write a book. So I did. The result was *Get Ready to Live! Living with Purpose and Passion*. It details not only the methods I used to overcome my alcohol addiction but also how to overcome fear and procrastination and how to find true purpose in life.

I am living proof that when a person has true purpose in life—purpose derived from an internal examination, not imposed by an outside force (whether it be religion, politics, education, tradition...anything external)—life becomes a happy challenge and each day is an enjoyable adventure. Today, I enjoy the occasional wine tasting and have never since felt like I needed a drink to get through the day. I happily live my life purpose every day and literally wake up excited to start my da

THE STORY OF PETER S.

My problems with alcohol began during my hitch in the Navy and continued for 26 years. Although there were plenty of problems and signs, the last year or so was undeniably the worst. I was failing at work, my personal life was a mess, and I kept getting in one scrape after another. Not legal scrapes, but I was doing the kinds of things that hurt other people, destroy your reputation, and cause a great deal of personal pain. Yes, the pain! And there was only one thing that would kill the pain, and unfortunately it was also the thing that caused more pain. And so on, and so on...until you reach the point where alcohol no longer kills the pain but you continue to drink anyway because it brings the relief of oblivion!

I convinced myself that all the pain I was in and all of my problems were due to my wife, my family, my job and in fact, just about everything in my life except, of course, myself. I made plans to escape to another part of the country, away from the things that were causing the pain. About a week before I was to leave in August of 1990, I had a rather emotional scene with my daughter. This experience enabled me to see myself and what I had become, clearer then anything ever had before.

The next day, I had lunch with my best friend and at 2:30 in the afternoon, over my last vodka martini, I told him that perhaps there was a possibility, that maybe I was drinking just a little bit too much. He told me that one of his other friends had gone to this "AA," where they had learned to drink like a normal person.

I made three phone calls from my car on the way home. The first was to my aunt who had been to treatment for alcoholism and was somewhat familiar with the 12-step program, which I thought was my only alternative. The second was to the AA hotline, which informed me of a meeting taking place near my home that evening, and the third was to my daughter, telling her to pour all of my booze down the sink. Having had a little time to think, I was convinced that I was through drinking. It wasn't worth it, I had had enough! I had reached the point the professionals call "crystallization of discontent." I finally connected the booze with the pain and the problems and realized that the costs of continuing to drink outweighed the benefits.

What I remember about the rest of the drive home was a feeling of tremendous relief that perhaps the nightmare was over. That feeling lasted until I actually got to the meeting that night, but I'll talk about that in a moment.

I arrived home all excited about my decision and couldn't wait to tell my wife about it. Far from sharing my relief, she was upset, obviously quite fearful of the consequences, and even tried to discourage me from going to the meeting. I didn't understand then that all she could see was the possibility of losing her 23-year drinking buddy and that she was asking herself if I would continue to put up with her drinking if I was sober. Nonetheless, I went to the meeting.

Walk into an AA meeting as a newcomer, as I did, and you will be told you have a terminal, incurable disease called alcoholism. Your only hope of arresting it and having any semblance of a normal life is to admit you are powerless over it and turn your will and your life over to a power greater than yourself, who is defined for you as "God as you understand Him." Your only other "choices" are jails, institutions or death. The people were nice, they seemed to understand and care about what I was going through, but I already knew I was done drinking; what was all this God stuff?

I went out for coffee after the meeting with a couple of guys who convinced me that if I didn't "take the suggestions," as they put it, I would shortly end up right back where I had been before. Well, I certainly didn't want to go back there, but I wasn't about to do any of the other stuff they suggested either. From the beginning, I didn't buy the "disease" model, or the higher power stuff. I never really got a sponsor, prayed or worked a step. What I did do was go to meetings—a lot of them. I first started going because it was an excuse to get out of the house, then it simply became another addiction. I didn't know about serotonin or the effects of "herding" then; I just knew I had to be there because I felt safe.

Had I known of any secular alternatives to AA or that it was possible to quit on my own, as 75% of all addicts do, I would have gone that route. As it was, I stuck with AA for a little over 10 years before leaving to start my own secular recovery meeting with a few friends. As it turns out, there are many routes to recovery from addiction and AA is one of the least effective for most people. *Alcoholics Anonymous*, the famous "Big Book," was written in 1939, when little, if anything, was known about addiction or the workings of the human mind itself. From then until now, neither a "jot nor tittle" of what Bill Wilson wrote in the first 164 pages has been changed in any way. That's really an astounding statement, when you consider all that has been learned about addiction in the last 70 years.

I feel I was one of those who stayed sober in spite of AA, not because of it.

SOBRIETY WITHOUT 12 STEPS

By Kelly Meister

I began drinking as a teenager, to numb the horror and agony of being repeatedly molested by a family member. While my underage friends drank with some moderation, I drank until I threw up or passed out, frequently with booze I had stolen from family members, neighbors and local stores. I spent over 10 years as a full-blown alcoholic. In my late 20s, depressed and desperate, I realized that the only thing alcohol was doing for me was making me suicidal. It was clear that I needed to quit.

I didn't have a plan in mind; I knew only that I needed to stop drinking. This alone wasn't the solution to my problems, it was merely a beginning. Shortly after I quit, I signed on with a therapist, the first of many I would see over the next 20 years. This first counselor said he didn't think that drinking was the problem but rather a symptom of the problem. In his estimation, if I addressed the fact of my molestation and the ensuing depression and poor self-esteem, then the drinking issue would take care of itself. While he turned out to be right about that, it wasn't an overnight fix. In reality, it would be many years before I developed healthy coping skills.

In the interim, I became involved with a crack addict. Conveniently, his addiction gave me a focus, and I spent several years trying to save him instead of taking care of myself. In disgust, when it became obvious that all those court-ordered rehabs weren't working, I started driving him to

12-step meetings and actually attending them, as well, to show him how it was done. I even had a sponsor for a time.

As much as I wanted to remain sober, it soon became obvious to me that there was a big problem with the 12-step community: They made it clear that you could never leave. At every single meeting—be it AA, NA, or CA—someone would speak up and insist that if you stopped coming to meetings, you would most assuredly start using again. Indeed, even in the 12 steps themselves there existed an escape clause: Step 3 says you must turn your life over to the care of God as you understand Him to be. In my view, this made for a very easy out when you relapsed: You could always say that, since you had turned your life over to Him, He allowed you to relapse instead of looking out for you.

The main thing that bothered me about the 12 steps, though, was that there was no room for personal growth. The steps only taught you how to get sober. They didn't teach you how to live sober, or deal with the problems that originally led to your addiction. There was no introspection required, beyond having to own up to the bad things you'd done while using.

In a way, this was probably a good thing: I attended enough meetings to see that the vast majority of participants appeared to be low-income and low intellect. For them, the 12 steps were probably a pretty simple formula, easy to follow and hard to screw up. The people I watched and heard at those meetings didn't seem to need or want more out of life than that. I did.

I never did develop a sobriety plan. I didn't realize that I needed one. What I did need, while involved with the crack addict and the dysfunctional relationships that followed, were practical, every-day ways to deal with the stress of life. I continued with therapy, plowing through six or seven specialists in a span of 20 years. Together, the experts and I focused on the molestation, the self-loathing, the depression. As my self-esteem improved, I no longer needed alcohol. I turned instead, to writing, finally putting together the book I had been meaning to write but never had the wherewithal to start. I added regular exercise to my agenda, and found that, not only did I enjoy all those walks at local parks, but I felt better physically, too. I bought myself a bicycle and peddled my stress away three seasons of the year. I started indulging my passion for art by getting out of the house and hitting area art shows. I started taking better care of myself all around.

Today, after all those years of therapy, I have an occasional drink in a restaurant and never feel the need to have a second or even finish the first. I no longer need to numb myself, or hide from the pain of the past. I have healthy coping skills in place to get me through the tough times, and it's been so long since I relied on alcohol that it never even occurs to me to reach for a drink now when I do encounter difficulties.

Given my experiences with the 12-step program, I am convinced that it's the beginning of sobriety, not the end. The 12 steps seem to work better for people of low to average IQs. Those with a more developed intellect would be better served doing individual therapy to examine and work through any childhood or traumatic issues. If insurance coverage is an issue, many areas of the country have county-run mental health services on a sliding-fee scale. No one is turned away because of inability to pay.

For those in doubt about their ability to make a better life for themselves, I say this: If I, a victim of incest and a former binge drinker, can create the life I was meant to live, then you can, too! There's so much to experience and enjoy when you're not enmeshed in the burden of addiction. It's not easy, and there's no simple, overnight fix, but if you want it badly enough, you, too, can live sober. So go for it! You've got nothing to lose!

LEAVING AA

By Deborah Dobson

I was in my late teens when I figured out that my parents were alcoholics. I'd read an article in a popular American magazine and suddenly, all the pieces of the confusing, often painful puzzle that was my family fell into place. Through a series of synchronistic events, I began attending Alateen several years later and went on to become very actively involved in other 12-step programs including Al Anon, ACOA (Adult Children of Alcoholics) and Emotions Anonymous. I chaired meetings, I spoke at meetings, I jumped in wholeheartedly because I'd finally found a home—a place where I was accepted and understood and where we could help each other get through the challenging daily struggles with our low self-esteem and feelings of victimization.

Back then, I truly believed that if I armed myself with enough information and went to enough meetings, I would never become an alcoholic like so many of my family members. But I was wrong. By the time I was in my late 30s, I was a daily drinker and I knew that if I didn't address this problem, it would only become worse. I reluctantly went to AA and started saying, "My name is Debby and I am an alcoholic."

Eventually, though, I again jumped in. AA became my new 12-step world and I grew to love the camaraderie, sharing my story and helping others.

In 1994, I moved from Connecticut to Arizona and immediately began attending AA meetings there. But I quickly discovered that they weren't the same and too often I found myself frustrated and leaving meetings feeling worse than I had when I arrived. I went through three sponsors in less than a year and saw a lot of behavior that I didn't think was "sober" or healthy emotionally, physically or spiritually.

After about a year, I finally stopped going to AA, but it was very difficult. I wrestled with a lot of fear (what if I relapsed?) and guilt (I wouldn't be there for others) and felt a tremendous sense of sadness and loss because 12-step programs had been my focus for over 20 years and had filled a very strong need in me to belong and be accepted.

Before I stopped going to AA though, I became aware that I wanted more. I knew my identity included more than just being an alcoholic and I wanted to expand the definition of my Self. I also wanted to spend my free time doing other things besides going to meetings. I wanted to volunteer in my community, I wanted to meet and spend time with people who didn't have addiction problems, I wanted to go on more hikes!

In hindsight, becoming disillusioned with AA in Arizona was probably the positive impetus that kicked me out of the 12-step "nest" and motivated me to actively begin seeking other solutions for recovery beyond those I'd already tried, such as individual and group therapy.

For some time, I'd questioned what AA said about my will versus "being willing." I knew I was willing to accept help and guidance, but I believed that without my own willpower, I would probably have relapsed. There were many times in early sobriety when I wanted to drink (back then, almost everything I encountered seemed like a crisis of overwhelming proportions and I had almost zero coping skills) and usually, there was no one around to stop me from acting on that desire. Ultimately, I always made a choice on my own not to pick up a drink—wasn't my will a part of that decision? Hadn't I been taught that people who succeeded used their will in a positive way to achieve success?

I began delving into many spiritual books, and I also wondered about the disease concept. If I had a disease and if other people had cured themselves of seemingly incurable diseases such as cancer, why couldn't I "cure" myself of alcoholism?

Another concept that many of the books I was reading advocated was how truly wonderful, creative and powerful we humans really are. If that was true, then why did we have to drink or act addictively at all? It was abundantly clear to me that I never again wanted to go down that dark path of excessive drinking, but I even wondered if I could teach myself to drink socially, something I still ponder today.

Over time, I developed an inner dialog: I would have a nonverbal mental conversation with myself and discuss the pros and cons of almost any major decision I was contemplating. When I had been sober almost 20 years, my beloved dog Nora was nearing the end of her life in the spring of 2010 and I would be lying if I said I didn't think about drinking to ease the pain and sadness of saying good-bye to her. But I also had a strong desire by then to emulate her: Even with all the challenges she'd faced in her early life (likely having been abused before I adopted her), she was an incredible power of example to me by her willingness to trust me, overcome her fears and grow into one of the most beautiful, loving beings I have ever known.

Becoming free of addiction, in all its forms (drinking, drugging, gambling, eating, relationships—there are so many!) is a personal goal of mine. As a human, I want to be as free as possible to enjoy the gift of life without the emotional and spiritual weight of lack of choice. I have not completely accomplished this yet, but the big ones are gone. Will I ever give up chocolate completely? No, but do I "need" it every day? No, and I don't want to need it; I want to enjoy and savor it as a delicious treat.

For me, the key to getting and staying sober was finding balance—getting enough sleep; making sure to supplement my diet with vitamins; making exercise part of my daily routine; figuring out what I enjoyed doing that really gave me joy and then doing it; asking for help and seeking answers when I got stuck; questioning the status quo; being humble and open enough to realize that I didn't have all the answers; not taking myself too seriously but respecting myself enough to not allow others to take me for granted; giving thanks during the day for all the gifts, large and small, I have been given; making time in my life to give back by volunteering for organizations I support in my community, which in turn makes me feel that I do indeed belong; recognizing and openly appreciating others for their time and for their talents and acknowledging and thanking others for opening themselves up to me and accepting me in their lives.

As of today, I have not had a drink for over 20 years and I rarely think about drinking. I heartily encourage you to invest in your wonderful Self, to seek out ways that work for you to become free of any addiction you may have. Think and seek outside the box, be an agent of life-affirming change and growth for yourself, for your community and for the world. Model that, share that and become a positive inspiration for others!

NOTES

NOTES

NOTES

Meet Hank Hayes the "agent of positive change."

Thank you so much for reading our book. We hope you have enjoyed it and found answers and solutions for yourself or your loved one.

Hank Hayes is available for live speaking events, OnTrack and Beyond seminars, motivational seminars, radio, television and other media interviews.

Don't miss the opportunity to have Mr. Hayes ruffle the feathers of your viewers and/or team. In a non-confrontational way, Hank gets you to see your own areas of needed improvement and helps create a fire inside to take action to better your own life utilizing his 5 master key formula.

Hank is a master of creating rapid results environments. He brings the same high energy and on-the-spot solutions to your event that he has to the military and law enforcement communities, where he's achieved life-saving results for decades!

Hank can be reached for booking at www.ontrackandbeyond.com or by phone at 484-393-1613.

9735275R0013

Made in the USA
Charleston, SC
07 October 2011